The Draconian Grimoires:

The Grimoire of the Sevenfold Serpent
7 Spells For 7 Sins
Tarot Magick For Fast Results
Powerful and Successful Witchcraft Spells
Fairy Household Magic
Ancient Spells With Clay
Dragon Magick of Merlin
Enochian Power Chants
How to Create a Golem
Ragnarok Magic
Rune Magic of the Norns (forthcoming)

RAGNAROK MAGIC

HARNESSING TRANSFORMATION FOR POSITIVE CHANGE

25 REAL LIFE APPLICATIONS AND SPELLS

by Jón Vaningi

3

4

THE DRACONIAN GRIMOIRES

The Draconian Grimoires are a series of powerful and instantly accessible and usable spell books and rituals based upon the system of Draconian Magic taught by Magister Michael Kelly in his series of books published by The Apophis Club.

Recently, Magister Kelly has spoken of the time when he first began studying magic, and the wonderful books of spells for immediate results magic which were then available. He expressed his desire to see such books return, so that newcomers to magic would have a means of learning the basics of magic very quickly and easily, through methods which bring rapid and definite results.

Magister Kelly is too busy with his series of advanced books for experienced initiates to write such spell books himself, but his words and hopes have given rise to this new series.

Whilst independent, this series of books is being produced with Magister Kelly's full knowledge and permission, and each manuscript is checked by him to ensure it is a proper fit with his system.

In this way, those magicians who find success with these easy and powerfully effective spells will be assured of the suitability of the more advanced titles of the Apophis Club (listed at the back of this book) should they wish to study more deeply.

WHAT IS DRACONIAN MAGIC?

Draconian Magic takes its name and theme from the ancient myths of the timeless, unformed Void which existed before the creation of the Universe, and will exist after the Universe ends.

The roots of consciousness were found in this Void in the shape of a gigantic Dragon. The desire of the Dragon to express itself led to the creation of the Universe, shaped out of the raw potential of the Void – where every possibility may be discovered – by the undulating, serpentine coils.

All that exists has been shaped from the nothingness of the Void (which only appears empty, but is actually full of potential for manifestation). And all that exists is suffused with the consciousness of the primordial Dragon. Our own consciousness, evolved over millions of years, is a tiny spark of the mind of this Eternal Serpent. We are truly the children of the Dragon.

Draconian Magic recognises the roots of our own selves in the Dragon and reaches back into the Void so that we can use it to shape new patterns into the fabric of the world, so that the things that we want will come to pass.

If you wish to see an excellent example of Draconian Magic in action, watch the film Excalibur, where the magician Merlin, played by Nicol Williamson, calls upon the Dragon to work his will in the world.

HOW MAGIC WORKS

The grimoires in this series are designed to get newcomers to magic successfully using spells to cause real changes in their lives. They have been trimmed back so that theory and philosophy is kept to a minimum and you can get straight into the work.

Because that's why anyone buys a book of magic spells in the first place, right? Because something in your life is unsatisfactory and you need to find a way to change it! If magic can't help you do that, what the hell is it for?

Nevertheless, there are some skills you will need to develop to make your magic as powerful as possible, so in this chapter I will tell you about them in as few words as possible, along with exercises which will help to develop and increase them.

Will

In order to get something through magic, you must exert your will upon it. The spells in this book will focus and direct your will, sending it on its course.

But first, of course, you need to know what you actually want. A vague notion is not enough. You must be able to define and state in clear, brief words exactly what you want and why. Being clear and concise about your desires brings your will into focus.

Will is not the same as 'willpower'. It is not straining your mind, with your eyes bulging with the effort. Will is a matter of thinking clearly about precisely what you want, with no vagueness or imprecision. Will is single-mindedness.

You can prepare your will to cast a spell by taking the time to consider what you want before you begin, until you can state it clearly and with absolute certainty in a single short sentence. Some examples will be given with each spell, but it's important to understand this main principle. A spell to "double my salary through either promotion or a better job" is likely to succeed, whereas "um... er... a little more money sometime might be nice" probably wouldn't achieve very much. Be precise and be sure of what you want, with no reservations.

Imagination

You also need to have a good imagination in order to successfully practice magic. Specifically, you should be able to visualise clearly.

The reason for this is that it is the imagination which is the conduit and the shaping force for magic. Look at the word, 'i-magi-nation'. Once you will has decided precisely what it is that you want, you must use your imagination to envision what it will be like when you get it. If you want a sexy lover, you must be able to imagine yourself with that hot lover in your arms (and your bed!). If you want riches, you must be able to imagine yourself living the good life, with a fine

8

home, a large bank balance, etc.

There are two reasons why this is important. The first is that if you cannot imagine yourself in a situation, perhaps you are overreaching your abilities. It has to be something which you can see as being possible, otherwise your subconscious – the part of your mind which links with the currents of the manifest world and reshapes them – will reject it. So you have to be able to conceive and fully imagine the results of your desired change in reality.

Secondly, your subconscious is best imprinted through images and it will look to the images you form within your imagination to determine what you really want and how you want it.

Some people say they have no imagination, or that they are not able to visualise. But many of them can, they just don't try hard enough. Ask them to remember one of their favourite memories, especially if it is one that excites the emotions and you'll find an image pops up pretty quick! When you visualise, it is the same thing in your reverse: with memories, your subconscious communicates with you by creating an image in your imagination; with visualisation, you communicate with your subconscious by doing the same, essentially what you are doing is trying to picture the memory of your glorious, magical future before it has yet happened. Understanding the process in this way can help some people break through their imaginative block.

However, there are a minority of people who really do struggle to use the visual imagination. If you are one of these people, you can still use your memories to discover the key to proceed. Even if you do not think visually, you still have memories. Recall a strong memory. Even if you don't have a visual image of it in your mind, take note of how it presents itself to you. How do you remember? Perhaps it is a mixture of sounds, words, or other sense impressions? Once you have analysed the way you access your memories and experience them, you have learned the method by which your subconscious communicates with you. Reverse engineer this, using the same impressions and sensations to imagine your willed goal, and that will be the most perfect way for you to communicate with your subconscious.

However you imagine, whether visually or otherwise, you will be glad to know that there are ways to improve and develop your abilities to an extraordinary degree.

Imagine an orange. At first it may be simple, a roughly circular shape of an orange colour. But then add all of the lovely texture of the peel and the slight variations in shade. Now you have added a tactile element to your imagination. Add to this by piercing the skin with your thumbnail and begin to peel the orange. Now you will also feel the texture of the inner flesh and the spurting juice. You will be able to smell that wonderful citrus aroma and to hear the sensual sound of the peel parting from the flesh. Your imagination may even be making your mouth water by this point. If so, this is great, as your imagination is having an actual physiological reaction. So raise that peeled imaginary orange up and take a bit. Imagine its intense flavour as its juices flood your mouth. And you know what? You are no longer simply 'visualising', you are now imagining with all five senses!

Practice this little exercise often, and you will be amazed how quickly it becomes so much more intense and 'real'. Developing this skill will pay huge dividends in the success of your magic!

Desire

It may seem extraordinary to have to say this, but you must make sure you actually want what you ask for when you use magic to obtain your wishes.

In other words, take time to determine what it is that you really want. This is really part of the 'will' process, but I am mentioning it here because it is so important.

Be aware of the consequences of obtaining your goals as well as the benefits. If you are dissatisfied with your income, are you ready for the upheaval and life changes that a new job or career, possibly necessitating a move, will entail? If you cast a spell to enchant someone to have sex with you, are you prepared to deal with the fallout, especially if you – or they – would be cheating? Once you have used magic to attract someone to you, they may well hang around if you want rid of them afterwards. Neither the spirits, nor the powers of the universe, nor your own unconscious will are going to be impressed if you then try to deny the magic you have done by trying to shake them loose. In fact, if you are that fickle, you may very well find your magic drying up in retribution.

So make sure you absolutely want what you ask for and are prepared to deal with the results practically when they happens.

But there is more to desire in magic than that. Once you have decided that you absolutely want something, you have to stoke that desire to a white heat. Emotion is the engine that drives magic, that powers it with sufficient force to being about change.

When you cast a spell, it must not be a flat, soulless recital of a few lines. You need to stir up your emotions and really pour your heart and soul into the performance of your spell if you want it to be effective. So spend a few minutes reasserting your will before you begin. Strongly imagine the result you want to happen. Then allow this imagination to arouse a strong emotional response. If you are working magic for money, gnash your teeth at your current lack and earnestly wish to be rich enough to afford the things you want. If you want love, your heart should be aching. If you want sex, you should be aflame with lust, feeling intense sexual excitement and longing. If you seek revenge for wrongs done to you, you should be enraged with hatred for your enemy. Take however

long it requires to ensure that this is so before
beginning.

Belief

It is very important that you focus all of your
concentrated will upon the performance of the ritual
and burn up all of your emotion in it, using your
intensity to fuel the spell. This will ensure that
when the spell has been cast and you close the
ritual and walk away, you will be able to let it go.

This does not mean that you will simply
'forget' about your ritual. How could you, if it is
something that is so important to you? But you
must no longer brood or fret about it. Instead, you
must deal with the world as if your requests have
already been granted. You must act in all
confidence that your magic has worked.

After all, if your spell is not even powerful
enough to calm your own doubts, how will it be
strong enough to alter the reality outside of
yourself? So you must exhibit absolute confidence
and when you think of the matter, it will be in a spirit
of certainty that it is being resolved to your
satisfaction.

Manifestation of Results

If you cast a spell to increase your money, it
is very unlikely that some stranger is simply going
to ring your doorbell carrying large bags of cash.
Magical results always take the easiest and most

13

accessible route when coming into manifestation.

We are surrounded by opportunities of all kinds at all times. But we are blinkered and do not see most of them, we are so absorbed in the everyday routines of our lives. Magic will often work by giving you a subconscious dig in the ribs that makes you spot a golden opportunity that you would otherwise have missed.

Perhaps you are in a dead end job and earning low wages, and you will be prompted by something that wells up from deep within yourself to apply for a position with a much better salary that you would normally have discounted. And then you get the job and your financial situation improves dramatically as a consequence. Or perhaps you will remember some collectibles that have lain gathering dust for years, but which a check on Ebay suggests may be worth many hundreds of pounds. Or people actually seem to enjoy the singing and guitar playing you indulge in as a hobby and are willing to pay money for that enjoyment. Three simple examples, but there are so many opportunities facing all of us every day that we simply do not notice until some 'hunch' – prompted by magic – draws our attention to them, with life-changing results.

If you are seeking love or sex, perhaps the only thing holding you back from scoring with that girl or boy you fancy is your own nervousness? We never measure up to those we find attractive in our own imaginations. But here's the thing: nor do they! And everyone's tastes are different.

Everyone is fancied by someone. It may be that magic will simply and suddenly fill you with the courage and self-confidence that you previously lacked, filling you with charisma and guiding you to speak just the right words to seem warm, witty and attractive.

A spell will sometimes work in a much more sudden and inexplicable way than these simple examples, producing results which are nothing short of miraculous. But as a general rule, the changes made will follow the path of least resistance, just as water will flow along well worn channels, only bursting the banks in a flood.

So always keep yourself alert after your spells. Be confident that the magic is working, but be ready to recognise and seize the opportunities that come your way as they arise, knowing that these are what you have asked for.

PART 1: SETTING THE STAGE FOR RAGNAROK MAGIC

Picture this: the world is ablaze, with flames leaping up and devouring everything in sight. The sky is filled with smoke and ash, obscuring the sun and casting the world into an eerie twilight. The oceans churn and boil, swallowing ships whole and tossing them like toys.

But it's not just the physical destruction that's happening here, folks. It's also a destruction of the old ways, the old order, the old gods. Everything is being swept away, torn down, and remade.

And yet, in the midst of all this destruction, there's a glimmer of hope. Because from the ashes of the old world, something new will rise. A new order, a new way of being, a new pantheon of gods.

So yes, Ragnarok is terrifying and devastating. But it's also a necessary step in the cycle of death and rebirth, and a reminder that even in the darkest of times, there's always the potential for something new and beautiful to emerge.

Let's talk about the destruction of Ragnarok, folks. It's like nothing you've ever seen before. We're talking about a cataclysmic event that shakes the very foundations of the world, and leaves nothing untouched.

First, let's talk about what it does to the world. The very earth shakes and quakes, as mountains crumble and oceans rise. The sky itself seems to be on fire, as flames consume everything in their path. It's like watching the apocalypse, folks, but on an even grander scale.

And what about the cosmos? That's right, the cosmos itself is affected by the destruction of Ragnarok. Stars fall from the sky, and the very fabric of space-time seems to be ripped apart at the seams. It's like watching the universe unravel before your very eyes.

But what about the individual? How does the destruction of Ragnarok affect the common man? Well, let me tell you, folks. It's like being reborn from the ashes. The old world is destroyed, and a new one is born in its place. It's like being given a second chance, a chance to start anew and make a better life for yourself.

So, there you have it, folks. The destruction of Ragnarok is a sight to behold, and one that will leave you breathless. But remember, even in the midst of destruction, there is always the possibility of rebirth and renewal.

Brief Introduction to Norse Mythology and Northern Magic

Norse mythology is a collection of stories and beliefs from the pre-Christian era of Northern Europe, primarily in what is now Scandinavia. These myths were passed down orally for centuries before being recorded in written form in medieval Iceland, and they have had a profound impact on the culture and history of the region.

One of the most important aspects of Norse mythology is its pantheon of gods and goddesses, which includes figures such as Odin, Thor, and Freyja. These deities each have their own personalities, powers, and stories, and they often interact with each other and with humans in complex ways.

Norse mythology also features a rich cast of other beings, such as giants, elves, and dwarves, and it includes a cosmology that explains the origins and nature of the universe.

Overall, Norse mythology has had a lasting impact on Western culture and has been a source of inspiration for literature, art, and popular culture. Its enduring popularity is a testament to the enduring power and appeal of its stories and characters.

The intersection of Norse Mythology and Northern Magic is a complex and deeply intertwined relationship that has been evolving for centuries.

Northern Magic is based on the belief that the natural world and the spiritual world are connected, and that by working with certain energies, you can create positive change in your life and in the world around you. Norse Mythology, on the other hand, is a collection of stories, myths, and legends that are central to the spiritual beliefs of the Nordic people.

Northern Magic draws heavily on the concepts and symbols found in Norse Mythology.

The runes, for example, are a key component of Northern Magic and have their roots in the mythology of Odin, the Norse god of wisdom and knowledge. The practice of *galdr*, which involves using sound to invoke certain energies or spirits, also has ties to Norse Mythology.

Many of the figures and concepts in Norse Mythology have been adopted by practitioners of Northern Magic as symbols of power and inspiration. The god Thor, for example, is often associated with strength and protection, while the goddess Freya is associated with love and fertility. The concept of the nine worlds, which is central to Norse Mythology, has also been incorporated into the practice of Northern Magic as a way of understanding the interconnectedness of all things.

Overall, the intersection of Norse Mythology and Northern Magic provides a rich and complex framework for spiritual practice and personal growth. By drawing on the wisdom and symbolism of these ancient traditions, practitioners of Northern Magic can tap into a deep well of power and inspiration that can help them to achieve their goals and create positive change in their lives and in the world around them.

Introduction to Ragnarok

Ragnarok is like the ultimate boss battle in Norse mythology. It's when the gods go to war with each other and everything we know is obliterated. But after the dust settles, there's a new beginning.

It's like hitting the reset button on the universe. In Northern Magic, people use this as a chance to transform themselves and achieve greater spiritual heights. It's a wake-up call to remind us that there's more to life than just the daily grind. It's a chance to shake things up and reach for the stars.

The Norse version of the apocalypse is no joke. It's like everything that could go wrong does go wrong. Even the big names like Odin, Thor, and Loki are wiped out. The Nine Worlds of Norse cosmology are gone too. It's like the ultimate disaster movie. But then, two humans survive and start over. It's like the ultimate reboot. And who doesn't love a good reboot?

Loki, that pesky trickster, had a hand in causing all of this destruction. It's as if he couldn't resist stirring the pot one last time. His actions set off a war between the gods and the giants that decimated everything in its path. Loki wanted to see how far he could push things before it all came crashing down. Well, he got his wish.

But even though everything is destroyed, it's not the end. It's more like a necessary step in a never-ending cycle of death and rebirth. Out with the old and in with the new. In Northern Magic, people use this as a chance to transform themselves on a personal and spiritual level. It's a way to let go of the past and embrace change. Like a phoenix rising from the ashes.

By embracing the teachings of Ragnarok,

people can learn to let go of old patterns and beliefs that may be holding them back. They get a chance to start afresh and move forward in a more positive direction. It's like the ultimate life lesson.

Origins and Evolution of Ragnarok

The myth of Ragnarok is a central theme in Norse mythology, describing the apocalyptic end of the world and the subsequent rebirth of a new world. The origins of the myth can be traced back to ancient Nordic and Germanic traditions, which featured concepts of cyclical destruction and regeneration.

The earliest mentions of Ragnarok can be found in the *Poetic Edda*, a collection of Old Norse poems written in the 13th century. These poems describe the events leading up to and following Ragnarok, including the battle between the gods and giants, the death of many gods and the eventual emergence of a new world.

The myth of Ragnarok has evolved over time, with various versions and interpretations emerging in different cultures and historical periods. In the Viking Age, for example, the myth was associated with a belief in a final battle between good and evil, with the outcome of the battle determining the fate of the world.

In more recent times, the myth of Ragnarok has been adapted and reinterpreted by various artists and writers, including J.R.R. Tolkien, who drew inspiration from Norse mythology for his *Lord of the Rings* trilogy. In popular culture, the concept of Ragnarok has also been featured in video games, movies, and television shows.

Overall, the myth of Ragnarok has endured over time due to its timeless themes of destruction and renewal, and its ability to inspire creative expression and interpretation in different cultural contexts.

CHAPTER 1: CREATION AND DESTRUCTION

Creation and destruction are two prominent themes in both Northern Magic and Norse mythology. In the beginning, Norse mythology describes the creation of the world through the collision of two worlds: Muspelheim, the land of fire, and Niflheim, the land of ice. The resulting explosion created the world we now know as Midgard, and the first humans, Ask and Embla, were created from two pieces of driftwood by the gods Odin, Vili, and Ve.

Similarly, creation and rebirth are also significant themes in Northern Magic, which views the world as a living organism that undergoes cycles of growth, decay, and rebirth. Practitioners of Northern Magic often seek to tap into the power of creation and harness it for personal growth and spiritual evolution.

On the other hand, destruction is also a significant theme in both Norse mythology and Northern Magic, exemplified by the cataclysmic events of Ragnarok. In Norse mythology, Ragnarok marks the end of the current world and the destruction of many gods and other beings. This destruction is also viewed as a necessary step towards the creation of a new world, with two humans surviving to start the cycle anew.

In Northern Magic, the concept of destruction is used as a means of shedding old patterns and beliefs to allow for new growth and transformation. This may involve confronting one's fears, letting go of the past, and embracing change. Practitioners of Northern Magic may also view destruction as a natural part of the universe's cyclical nature and seek to harness its power for personal transformation.

Overall, the themes of creation and destruction in Northern Magic and Norse mythology reflect the cyclical nature of life and the importance of change and transformation for personal growth and spiritual evolution.

Norse creation myth and its parallels with Ragnarok

The Norse creation myth tells the story of how the world came into being. In the beginning, there was a vast, dark void known as Ginnungagap. To the north was the frozen land of Niflheim, and to the south was the fiery land of Muspelheim. The two lands eventually met in the middle, where they created a giant named Ymir.

Ymir was the first of the giants, and from his body, the gods created the world. Odin, Vili, and Ve killed Ymir and used his body to create the earth, the sky, and the sea. They used his bones to create mountains, his blood to create the oceans, and his skull to create the dome of the sky.

This creation myth has parallels with the story of Ragnarok, which tells of the end of the world. In both stories, there is a sense of cyclical destruction and rebirth. In the creation myth, Ymir's death leads to the creation of the world. In

Ragnarok, the world is destroyed so that a new world can be born.

Another parallel between the two stories is the idea of a battle between gods and giants. In the creation myth, Ymir is a giant, and the gods create the world by defeating him. In Ragnarok, the giants and the gods engage in a final battle that leads to the destruction of the world.

Additionally, both stories feature a theme of sacrifice. In the creation myth, the gods sacrifice Ymir to create the world. In Ragnarok, many of the gods die in battle, sacrificing themselves for the greater good and paving the way for the rebirth of the world.

Overall, the Norse creation myth and the myth of Ragnarok are intertwined, both featuring themes of creation and destruction, cyclical rebirth, battles between gods and giants, and the importance of sacrifice.

Cycles of creation and destruction

In Norse mythology, the concept of cycles of creation and destruction is central. This is illustrated in the story of creation, where the giant Ymir is slain by the gods and his body is used to create the world as we know it. This act of destruction leads to a new creation, with the gods and humans living in a new, better world.

The idea of cycles of creation and destruction is also seen in the myth of Ragnarok.

This is a time of great upheaval, when the gods battle each other and the world is destroyed. However, this destruction paves the way for a new world to emerge, with two humans surviving and repopulating the world.

In Northern Magic, the concept of cycles of creation and destruction is seen as a powerful reminder of the need for change and growth. The story of Ragnarok serves as a symbol of personal transformation, where the destruction of the old world allows for new beginnings and fresh starts.

An inspiring modern story that illustrates this concept is that of a young woman named Olivia. Olivia had struggled with addiction and had hit rock bottom, feeling like there was no way out of the cycle of destruction that she had found herself in. However, through the practice of Northern Magic, Olivia learned to embrace the idea of cycles of creation and destruction.

She recognized that the destruction of her old way of life was necessary in order to create a new, better version of herself. With the help of the teachings of Northern Magic, Olivia was able to let go of her old habits and beliefs and start anew. She found strength and resilience in the knowledge that destruction is not an ending, but rather a necessary step towards renewal and growth.

Olivia's story is a powerful reminder that cycles of creation and destruction are not something to be feared, but rather embraced as a necessary part of personal transformation and growth. By recognizing the need for change and being willing to let go of the old in order to make way for the new, we can all find the strength to create a better, more fulfilling life for ourselves.

Yggdrasil, the World Tree, and Ragnarok

Yggdrasil, the World Tree, is a central figure in Norse mythology and is intricately linked to the concept of Ragnarok. In Norse cosmology, Yggdrasil is a massive yew tree that connects the Nine Worlds of the cosmos. It is considered the *axis mundi*, or the center of the universe, and serves as a bridge between the gods, the giants, and humanity.

During the events of Ragnarok, Yggdrasil is subjected to immense destruction along with the rest of the cosmos. It is said that the tree will shake and groan under the weight of the battle, and its roots will be torn asunder. Despite the devastation, however, it is believed that Yggdrasil will survive the cataclysmic event and play a crucial role in the renewal of the world.

The importance of Yggdrasil in the context of Ragnarok lies in its symbolic significance. The tree represents the interconnectedness of all things in the cosmos and serves as a reminder that even in the face of destruction and chaos, there is always the possibility of rebirth and renewal.

For practitioners of Northern Magic, the World Tree is a powerful symbol that can help them connect with the cyclical nature of creation and destruction. By meditating on the image of Yggdrasil, they can gain a deeper understanding of the interconnectedness of all things and the importance of letting go of the old in order to make way for the new.

An inspiring modern story that illustrates the concepts of Yggdrasil and cycles of creation and destruction is the tale of a woman who experienced a devastating loss in her life. She had lost her job, her marriage had ended, and she was struggling to find her place in the world.

Feeling lost and alone, she turned to the teachings of Northern Magic and began meditating on the image of Yggdrasil. Through her practice, she gained a deeper understanding of the cyclical nature of life and the importance of letting go of the past in order to move forward.

Slowly but surely, the woman began to rebuild her life. She found a new job that she enjoyed, made new friends, and started pursuing hobbies and interests that she had neglected for years. Although she still carried the pain of her past, she realized that it no longer defined her and that she had the power to create a new life for herself.

Through her experience, the woman came to understand the importance of embracing the cycles of creation and destruction in her own life. Like Yggdrasil, she had weathered the storm of destruction and was now ready to embrace the

28

renewal that comes with new beginnings.

CHAPTER 2: THE PROPHESIED EVENTS OF RAGNAROK

As the day of Ragnarok draws closer, the world awaits the prophesied events that will mark the end of the current cycle of existence. Many have come to view this catastrophic event as a time of great upheaval and destruction, a time when the gods will battle each other and the world as we know it will be destroyed. However, there are those who believe that the Ragnarok is not just a time of endings, but a time of new beginnings.

One such person is a young man named Erik, who grew up in a small town in Norway. Erik was an average young man, leading an unremarkable life until a harrowing experience changed everything for him. One night, as Erik was walking home from work, he saw a bright light in the sky. As he gazed up at the light, he felt an overwhelming sense of fear and dread wash over him. Suddenly, the ground beneath his feet began to shake, and he heard a deafening roar as if the world itself was coming apart.

In that moment, Erik felt a deep sense of terror and despair, convinced that the end of the world was upon him. But as he continued to stand there, frozen in fear, he began to feel a strange sense of calm wash over him. It was as if a weight had been lifted from his shoulders, and he realized that this moment of destruction was also a moment of rebirth.

As he walked home that night, Erik couldn't shake the feeling that he had just witnessed a small taste of the events of Ragnarok. Over the coming days and weeks, he began to delve deeper into the myths and legends of Norse mythology, seeking to understand the significance of what he had experienced.

What he discovered was a rich tapestry of stories and teachings that spoke to the cyclical nature of existence, where death and destruction are not the end but merely the precursor to new beginnings. Inspired by these teachings, Erik began to practice Northern Magic, using the prophesied events of Ragnarok as a powerful symbol to represent personal transformation and growth.

Years later, Erik had become a respected practitioner of Northern Magic, helping others to embrace the teachings of Ragnarok and find meaning and purpose in the cycles of creation and destruction. His own experience of witnessing a small taste of Ragnarok had led him on a journey of self-discovery and personal transformation, ultimately leading him to a deeper understanding of the world and his place in it.

Events leading up to Ragnarok

According to Norse mythology, several prophesied events will occur before the onset of Ragnarok. These events will signal the coming of the apocalyptic battle and the destruction of the world as we know it. Here is an overview of some of these prophesied events:

Fimbulwinter is a period of great cold, darkness, and hardship that is prophesied to precede Ragnarok, the end of the world in Norse mythology. It is said to last for three consecutive years without any intervening summers, with the sun and moon disappearing from the sky, and harsh winds and snowstorms battering the land.

During Fimbulwinter, food and resources become scarce, and people struggle to survive in the harsh conditions. Many people perish due to the extreme cold, hunger, and disease that accompany the winter. It is said that even the gods will suffer during this time, with many of them being killed or incapacitated in the lead-up to Ragnarok.

The intense and prolonged nature of Fimbulwinter is significant because it serves as a precursor to the ultimate destruction that will follow during Ragnarok. This period of hardship and suffering is seen as a necessary prelude to the end of the world, as it represents a time of testing and purification for those who will survive the coming cataclysm. It is only through enduring the trials of Fimbulwinter that one can hope to emerge strong enough to face the challenges of the coming Ragnarok.

In Northern Magic, Fimbulwinter is viewed as an opportunity for personal growth and spiritual transformation. By enduring the hardships of this time, individuals can learn to cultivate inner strength, resilience, and self-reliance, qualities that

32

will be essential for survival during the tumultuous events of Ragnarok. It is said that those who are able to withstand the trials of Fimbulwinter will be better prepared to face the ultimate test of Ragnarok and emerge stronger and wiser for it.

In Norse mythology, the **three roosters** play a significant role in signaling the beginning of the end times, or Ragnarok. These roosters are said to be located in different realms of the cosmos, with each crowing at a specific time to signal the coming of the apocalypse.

The first rooster, named Gullinkambi, is located in the underworld of Hel. According to legend, Gullinkambi will wake the dead with its crowing, summoning all of the fallen warriors to join the final battle at Ragnarok.

The second rooster, named Fjalar, is located in Jotunheim, the world of the giants. When Fjalar crows, it signals the beginning of the end of the world and the start of the battle between the gods and the giants.

The last rooster, named Víðópnir, is located in the world of humans, Midgard. Its crowing will signal the beginning of Fimbulwinter, the three-year winter that precedes Ragnarok.

The crowing of the three roosters represents the coming together of the different realms of the cosmos, signaling the end of the current world and the start of a new one. The roosters serve as powerful symbols of the interconnectedness of all things, reminding us of the cyclical nature of life and the inevitability of change.

In Norse mythology, **Fenrir** is the son of the trickster god Loki and the giantess Angrboda. The birth of Fenrir is one of the most foreboding signs of Ragnarok, as he is destined to bring about the destruction of the world. According to the myth, the gods became alarmed at Fenrir's rapid growth and bound him with a magical chain known as Gleipnir. But as Fenrir grew stronger, he was able to break free from his chains, unleashing chaos upon the world.

Fenrir is depicted as a monstrous wolf with insatiable appetite and a fierce demeanor. His appearance is often associated with darkness, and he is feared for his ability to devour everything in his path. In some versions of the myth, Fenrir is said to have a gaping maw that can swallow the sun and the moon, plunging the world into an eternal darkness.

The birth and growth of Fenrir is seen as a warning of the dangers of unbridled power and unchecked growth. In the context of Northern Magic, it serves as a metaphor for the destructive forces that can arise when we allow our negative impulses to run wild. The story of Fenrir reminds us of the importance of temperance and self-control, and the need to recognize our own capacity for destruction.

In Norse mythology, **Naglfar** is a ship that is made from the fingernails and toenails of the dead. According to the myth, the ship is owned by the giant Hymir, and during the time of Ragnarok, Naglfar will set sail from its moorings, piloted by the god Loki, who has joined forces with the giants. The ship's appearance in the waters is seen as an omen of impending doom and the arrival of the end of the world.

The idea of the Naglfar has been interpreted by scholars in various ways, with some seeing it as a metaphor for the ultimate degradation of humanity and the futility of resistance against the forces of chaos and destruction. Others view it as a symbol of the inevitability of death and the cyclical nature of existence, where everything that is born must eventually die and return to the earth.

In Northern Magic, the symbolism of the Naglfar is often used to represent the need for individuals to confront their fears and to be prepared for the challenges that life can bring. The Naglfar is seen as a reminder that life is fleeting and that we must make the most of the time that we have. At the same time, it is also a symbol of hope, as it suggests that new beginnings can emerge from the ashes of the old.

For example, a person who is facing a difficult time in their life may see the Naglfar as a symbol of the obstacles that they must overcome in order to reach a better place. By facing their fears and taking on the challenge, they can emerge stronger and more resilient, ready to face whatever the future may hold. In this way, the Naglfar can inspire individuals to take control of their lives and to embrace the transformative power of change.

The **War of the Gods** is the ultimate and final battle between the deities and their foes, the giants, which will determine the fate of the cosmos. This catastrophic event is predicted to be characterized by the most intense and terrifying struggle imaginable, with the sky itself shuddering and cracking, the ground shaking, and the world quaking under the strain of the battle.

The giants and their armies will emerge from all corners of the world, ready to destroy everything in their path, including the gods and their followers. The gods will also be ready, prepared for this final battle that they have known would come for eons. The legendary figures of Norse mythology, including Odin, Thor, and Freyja, will fight bravely alongside their followers, making their final stand against the giants.

The War of the Gods will be a brutal and bloody affair, with both sides sustaining immense losses. The gods will be facing their ultimate doom, as they know that their victory will be short-lived and that they will ultimately be defeated. Nonetheless, they fight on, driven by their sense of duty and their determination to defend their world, even if it means sacrificing themselves in the process.

The outcome of the battle is uncertain, and the final moments of the gods will be closely watched by the surviving humans who will go on to repopulate the earth after the destruction of Ragnarok. Nonetheless, despite the bleak outlook, there is a sense of optimism and renewal at the end of the battle, as it is believed that the world will be reborn from the ashes of the old one.

Indeed, the events leading up to Ragnarok may seem like a bleak outlook for the world, but for the Norse, it was viewed as a natural cycle of destruction and regeneration. The end of the world was not seen as an ending, but rather a necessary step in the cyclical process of life. The idea of destruction and rebirth can be seen in many aspects of Norse mythology, from the birth of the world through the sacrifice of Ymir to the eventual rebirth of the world after Ragnarok.

Furthermore, the concept of the cycle of destruction and regeneration can also be applied to our own lives. Just as the world goes through periods of destruction and regeneration, we too can experience hardships and challenges that ultimately lead to growth and new beginnings. The story of Ragnarok serves as a reminder that even in the face of destruction, there is always the potential for rebirth and renewal.

Key figures of Ragnarok

In Norse mythology, the key figures play significant roles in the events leading up to Ragnarok. Here are some of the key figures and their roles:

Odin

Odin is considered the god of wisdom, war, and death. He is the Allfather and ruler of the gods in

Asgard. Odin is one of the most complex figures in Norse mythology, and his role in Ragnarok is multifaceted. He is the one who gains knowledge of the coming events and attempts to prepare his warriors for the battle ahead. Odin's sacrifice of his eye to Mimir's well in exchange for wisdom is symbolic of his willingness to do whatever it takes to prepare for the end times.

In addition to being the god of wisdom, war, and death, Odin is also known as the god of poetry, magic, and prophecy. He is said to have sacrificed himself to himself by hanging himself on the world tree, Yggdrasil, for nine days and nights to gain knowledge of the runes, which are symbols used for magic and divination.

Odin is often depicted as a wise and powerful figure, but he is also known for his cunning and devious nature. He frequently employs trickery and manipulation to achieve his goals, even if it means sacrificing the lives of others. This complexity is reflected in his role in Ragnarok, where he must balance his desire to win the war with his knowledge of the ultimate fate of the world.

Despite his flaws, Odin is revered as the Allfather and ruler of the gods, and his wisdom and sacrifices are seen as necessary for the survival of the Norse gods and the continuation of the cycle of creation and destruction.

Thor

Thor is the god of thunder and is known for his strength and bravery. He is the defender of Asgard and the enemy of the giants. Thor's role in Ragnarok is to battle against the monstrous serpent Jormungand and to fight alongside the other gods against the giants.

Thor is one of the most beloved gods in Norse mythology, revered for his strength, courage, and unwavering loyalty to his fellow gods. He is known as the god of thunder, wielding his hammer Mjolnir to summon lightning bolts and storms. Thor's role in Ragnarok is crucial, as he is tasked with battling the monstrous serpent Jormungand, who has been a recurring antagonist throughout Norse mythology. According to the myth, Thor and Jormungand will fight to the death, with both ultimately perishing in the battle.

Thor is also a key player in the final battle against the giants, as he uses his mighty hammer to crush his enemies and protect the gods of Asgard. His bravery and strength in battle make him a formidable opponent, and he is highly respected and admired among the gods and the people of Midgard. In many ways, Thor represents the ideals of strength and courage that were highly valued in Norse culture, and his role in Ragnarok reflects the importance of standing up against one's enemies, no matter how daunting the challenge may seem.

Loki

Loki is a complex figure in Norse mythology, known for his trickster nature and cunning. He is the son of two giants but is also considered a god. Loki's role in Ragnarok is to be the catalyst for the events that lead to the end of the world. He is responsible for the release of Fenrir and the death of Balder, which leads to the beginning of the end times. Loki ultimately fights against Heimdall and kills him before being killed himself by the god Vidar.

Loki's role in Ragnarok is significant as he is seen as the embodiment of chaos and disruption. His trickster nature and unpredictable behavior make him both a valuable ally and a dangerous enemy. In Norse mythology, Loki's actions often lead to unintended consequences and his involvement in the events leading up to Ragnarok is no different. His actions ultimately lead to the destruction of the world and the downfall of the gods.

However, it is worth noting that Loki's character is not entirely negative, as he also brings about positive change and transformation in some myths. For example, he helps the gods retrieve Thor's stolen hammer and is instrumental in the creation of the walls of Asgard. In some interpretations, Loki is seen as a symbol of the transformative power of chaos and the potential for positive change that can come from destruction and upheaval.

Despite his complex role in the myth of Ragnarok, Loki remains a popular figure in modern culture and continues to inspire adaptations and interpretations in literature, film, and other forms of media.

Freyja

Freyja is the goddess of love, fertility, and war. She is one of the most powerful goddesses in Norse mythology and is associated with the afterlife. Freyja's role is to lead the Valkyries into battle and to choose half of the slain warriors.

In addition to her role in battle, Freyja also has a personal stake in the events of Ragnarok. According to some versions of the myth, Freyja's brother Freyr will die in battle against the giant Surt. Freyja is said to weep tears of gold for her fallen brother, demonstrating the depth of her emotional connection to those she loves.

Freyja's association with the afterlife is also significant in the context of Ragnarok. As the leader of the Valkyries, she has the power to choose which fallen warriors will be taken to Valhalla to prepare for the final battle. Her role as a goddess of love and fertility is also connected to the idea of regeneration and rebirth, which is a key theme in the cyclical nature of Norse mythology. Overall, Freyja's multifaceted role in Norse mythology underscores the interconnectedness of different aspects of life and death, love and war, and the natural cycles of the world.

Heimdall

Heimdall is the god of light, guardian of the Bifrost Bridge, and is known for his ability to see and hear all. Heimdall's role in Ragnarok is to blow the Gjallarhorn to signal the beginning of the final battle and to fight against Loki.

41

Heimdall's role in Ragnarok is crucial as he serves as the guardian of Asgard and the one who is responsible for detecting any potential threat to the realm. It is said that he can see and hear everything that happens in the nine worlds and possesses incredible senses. He is known for his sharp eyesight and can see great distances, even in complete darkness. Heimdall is also responsible for guarding the Bifrost Bridge, the rainbow bridge that connects Asgard with the other realms.

During Ragnarok, Heimdall's duty is to blow the Gjallarhorn, a powerful horn that can be heard throughout the universe, to signal the beginning of the final battle. He is also a key player in the War of the Gods, where he fights against Loki, the god responsible for bringing about the end of the world. Heimdall's death at the hands of Loki is a significant event in the myth, as it is one of the final battles before the ultimate destruction of the world.

Recap of Roles

The roles and significance of these key figures in the myth of Ragnarok reveal the complexity and depth of Norse mythology. Each character embodies different traits and plays a significant role in the events that lead up to the end of the world, highlighting the cyclical nature of creation and destruction in Norse mythology.

Odin, the Allfather, represents wisdom, knowledge, and sacrifice. He is responsible for preparing his warriors for the final battle and gaining knowledge of the coming events.

Thor, the defender of Asgard, represents strength, bravery, and loyalty. He is the defender of the gods against the giants and is tasked with fighting against the monstrous serpent Jormungand.

Loki, the trickster, embodies chaos, cunning, and betrayal. His role as a catalyst for the events leading to the end of the world highlights the unpredictability of life and the inevitability of change.

Freyja, the goddess of love, fertility, and war, represents the power of femininity and the afterlife. Her role as a leader of the Valkyries and chooser of the slain emphasizes the importance of valuing life and death equally.

Heimdall, the god of light and the guardian of the Bifrost Bridge, represents vigilance, protection, and foresight. His ability to see and hear all, as well as his role in blowing the Gjallarhorn, signifies the importance of awareness and preparedness for change.

Together, these characters and their roles demonstrate the multifaceted nature of Norse mythology, highlighting the interconnectedness of life, death, and regeneration.

Modern Use Example

The battle between the gods and the giants in the myth of Ragnarok is a significant event that symbolizes the ultimate conflict between good and evil. It represents the struggle between order and chaos, with the gods fighting to preserve their realm and the giants seeking to bring about its destruction.

To illustrate the power of the gods over the giants, consider a modern story in which a group of travelers find themselves stranded in a remote area during a powerful blizzard. They take refuge in an old cabin, but as the night wears on, they realize they are not alone. Outside, they hear the sounds of giants pounding on the door, demanding entry.

As the travelers huddle together in fear, an old woman appears before them, dressed in furs and carrying a staff. She introduces herself as a practitioner of Northern magic, skilled in the ancient ways of the gods. With her help, the travelers begin to prepare themselves for battle.

The old woman teaches them how to invoke the power of the gods, calling upon Thor to imbue their weapons with lightning, Freyja to grant them courage and strength, and Odin to give them wisdom and cunning. Together, they create a circle of protection around the cabin, using ancient runes to ward off the giants' attacks.

As the night wears on, the giants become more desperate, hurling boulders and tree trunks at the cabin. But the travelers stand firm, wielding their enchanted weapons with skill and determination. With the power of the gods behind them, they are able to withstand the giants' onslaught, ultimately driving them back into the wilderness.

In this modern story, the power of Northern magic demonstrates the strength and resilience of the gods in the face of adversity – and humans in the face of the blizzard. It highlights the importance of courage, wisdom, and strength in the face of evil, and emphasizes the enduring significance of the gods and their mythological battles against the forces of chaos and destruction.

CHAPTER 3: THE AFTERMATH OF RAGNAROK

The aftermath of Ragnarok is a crucial part of the myth, and let me tell you, it's a doozy. After all the craziness of the gods battling the giants and the world being destroyed, a new world emerges from the ashes. And get this - the gods who survived and a handful of humans who sheltered in the world-tree Yggdrasil's trunk are the ones who make it out alive.

Once they emerge from their hiding places, they have to figure out how to rebuild their world. So, they come together and discuss what they need to do to start anew. And thus begins the Golden Age, a time of peace and prosperity. It's said that this new world is even more beautiful than the old one, and the survivors are grateful for the fresh start.

So, what does this all mean? Well, my friends, it's all about the cyclical nature of creation and destruction in Norse mythology. Nothing lasts forever, and everything is subject to change. But even when everything is destroyed, there is always the hope of a new beginning, a chance to start over and make things better.

And that, my friends, is the power of the myth of Ragnarok. It teaches us that even when everything seems hopeless and the end is near, there is always the possibility of a new beginning. So, embrace change, my friends, and never lose hope for a brighter tomorrow.

Positive Points

When we look at the myth of Ragnarok, we see a pretty compelling message about the cycle of destruction and rebirth. The idea that everything is subject to change and that even the gods themselves must eventually face the ultimate reckoning is a sobering one.

But there's also a sense of hope that comes with the destruction and rebirth depicted in the myth. The idea that a new beginning is possible, even after the most catastrophic of events, is a powerful one. It reminds us that even in the darkest of times, there is always the possibility of renewal.

In many ways, the myth of Ragnarok speaks to the human experience. We all face challenges and setbacks in our lives, and there are times when it can feel like everything is falling apart. But if we can hold on to the idea that destruction can be followed by rebirth, then we can find the strength to persevere.

So, while the destruction depicted in the myth of Ragnarok may be terrifying, it is also a reminder that new beginnings are possible. And in a world where change is constant, that's a message that we can all take to heart.

Once there was a woman named Jasmine who had struggled with her weight for years. She had tried every fad diet and exercise regimen under the sun but had never been able to stick to anything long enough to see results. Jasmine had resigned herself to a life of being overweight and unhappy.

One day, Jasmine was walking through the park and saw a butterfly emerging from its cocoon. She watched in amazement as the butterfly struggled to free itself from its confines, eventually breaking free and spreading its wings. Jasmine was struck by the beauty of the butterfly and realized that it was a symbol of new beginnings and transformation.

Inspired by the butterfly's journey, Jasmine decided to make a change. She started by taking small steps, like cutting back on sugary drinks and taking short walks each day. As she began to see results, Jasmine became more motivated to continue her journey.

With time, Jasmine lost weight and regained her confidence. She felt like a new person, free from the weight that had held her back for so long. Jasmine realized that new beginnings were possible, and that she had the power to transform her life.

The story of Jasmine shows that new beginnings are possible, no matter how difficult or impossible they may seem at first. Just like the butterfly emerging from its cocoon, we too can break free from our confines and transform ourselves into something new and beautiful. All it takes is the courage to take that first step and the determination to keep going, even when the journey gets tough.

"New World" Emerging

What are the practical implications of this idea of a "New World" emerging after the end of the old?

One day, a young woman found herself overwhelmed by stress at work. She was constantly worried about meeting deadlines, pleasing her boss, and keeping up with the demands of her job. The pressure was taking a toll on her mental and physical health, and she knew she needed to find a way to reduce her stress levels.

One evening, while sitting at home, she decided to take a few minutes to envision a better future for herself. She closed her eyes and imagined a life where she had a fulfilling career, a happy family, and enough free time to pursue her hobbies and passions. She pictured herself waking up every day feeling energized and excited about the day ahead, and going to bed every night with a sense of accomplishment and contentment.

As she visualized this future, she felt a sense of calm and peace wash over her. She realized that the stress she was feeling was just a temporary obstacle, and that she had the power to create a better life for herself.

Over time, the young woman continued to focus on her vision of a better future. She took small steps towards her goals, such as taking breaks during the workday to go for a walk or to meditate, and setting boundaries with her boss to ensure that her workload was manageable.

49

Slowly but surely, the stress began to lift, and she felt more empowered and in control of her life. By envisioning a better future for herself and taking action to make it a reality, she found a new beginning and a new sense of purpose and fulfillment.

Symbolic sacrifice

The myth of Ragnarok is rich with symbolic meanings that have resonated with people for centuries. One of the most significant themes is the cyclical nature of life. The idea that destruction and rebirth are part of the natural order of things is a fundamental aspect of Norse mythology. It's a reminder that even the most terrible events can lead to new beginnings.

Another important theme is the idea of sacrifice. In Norse mythology, sacrifice is essential for the gods to maintain their power and keep the world in balance. Odin's sacrifice of his eye and hanging on the world tree are examples of this. Sacrifice is a difficult concept for many of us, but it can be a powerful reminder that sometimes we have to give up something in the present to secure a better future.

Let me give you an example of how sacrifice can play out in someone's life. Imagine a working mother who wants to advance her career but also wants to be present for her children. She may have to sacrifice some of her free time to study for a certification that will help her get ahead at work. Or

50

she may have to miss her child's soccer game to attend an important meeting. Sacrifice in this context means making difficult choices to achieve her goals while still being a good parent.

By embracing the idea of sacrifice, the working mother can envision a better future for herself and her family. She knows that the sacrifices she makes now will pay off in the long run. In this way, the myth of Ragnarok can serve as a reminder that sometimes, we have to give up something in the present to secure a better future.

Similarly, on the theme of sacrifice, let me tell you a story about a young man named Mike. He found himself divorced and paying child support for his daughter, Lily. Mike was devastated by the breakup of his marriage, but he knew that he had to do what was best for his child.

Mike understood that he needed to make sacrifices to ensure that his daughter had a good life. He worked long hours at his job to provide for Lily's needs, often sacrificing his own free time and social life to spend time with her. He also made sure to be there for all of her important milestones, such as school performances, birthdays, and sports games.

Mike's sacrifices were not always easy, but he persevered through them because he loved his daughter and wanted to give her the best life possible. He saw his role as a father as a sacred duty, and he would do whatever it took to fulfill that duty.

In many ways, Mike's sacrifices mirrored those of the Norse god Odin. Odin gave up one of his eyes to gain wisdom and knowledge and even sacrificed himself by hanging from the world-tree Yggdrasil to gain knowledge of the runes. Similarly, Mike sacrificed his own desires and free time to provide for his daughter, and he saw this sacrifice as a way to gain wisdom and knowledge about the importance of being a good father.

In the end, Mike's sacrifices paid off, as Lily grew up to be a happy, well-adjusted young woman who loved her father deeply. Mike's sacrifices may not have been on the grand scale of the gods of Norse mythology, but they were just as heroic and inspiring, and they show the importance of sacrifice in creating a better future for our loved ones.

CHAPTER 4: CULTURAL SIGNIFICANCE OF RAGNAROK

Ragnarok is not just a myth, but it also holds significant cultural importance in Norse history and mythology. It is a representation of the cyclical nature of life and death, destruction and creation. The myth is a reminder that nothing lasts forever, and everything is subject to change.

The cultural significance of Ragnarok is evident in the fact that it has been retold and adapted in various forms of media, from literature to movies and video games. Its themes of sacrifice, rebirth, and renewal continue to resonate with audiences today.

Additionally, the myth plays an essential role in the identity and beliefs of modern Norse pagans and Asatru practitioners. For them, Ragnarok is not just a story but a part of their religious worldview. They see the myth as a representation of the cycles of life, death, and rebirth and a reminder of the importance of living in harmony with nature.

In conclusion, the myth of Ragnarok is not just a tale of gods and giants battling it out, but it is a representation of the cycle of life and death, destruction and creation. Its cultural significance is evident in its widespread retelling and adaptation in various forms of media and its importance in modern Norse paganism and Asatru practices.

Historical context

When we look at the historical context in which the myth of Ragnarok emerged, we see a society that was deeply connected to the natural world and its cycles. The Norse people were farmers and hunters, and their livelihoods depended on the changing of the seasons and the cycles of life and death.

In this context, the myth of Ragnarok can be seen as a reflection of the Norse people's understanding of the cyclical nature of life and death. It speaks to their belief that nothing lasts forever and that everything is subject to change. It also reflects their worldview, which was deeply rooted in the idea of fate and the idea that certain events were predetermined.

Moreover, the myth of Ragnarok emerged during a time of great political and social upheaval in Norse society. The Viking Age was marked by raids, migrations, and the consolidation of power by various leaders and kingdoms. In this context, the myth can be seen as a way of coping with the uncertainty and chaos of the times.

In summary, the myth of Ragnarok emerged from a society that was deeply connected to the natural world and its cycles, and that was also experiencing significant political and social upheaval. It reflects the Norse people's understanding of the cyclical nature of life and death, their belief in fate, and their need to make sense of the uncertainty and chaos of their times.

Cultural Influence

The myth of Ragnarok has had a profound influence on Norse culture and subsequent generations. It has shaped the way the Norse people viewed the world, life, death, and the afterlife. The myth provided a framework for understanding the cyclical nature of life and the inevitability of destruction and rebirth. It also emphasized the importance of bravery, sacrifice, and loyalty to one's people and gods.

The myth's influence can be seen in various aspects of Norse culture, including their religious beliefs, literature, art, and even political and social structures. The Norse people believed that death was not the end, but rather a transition to the afterlife, where they could continue to live with their gods and ancestors.

Furthermore, the myth of Ragnarok has inspired countless works of literature, art, and popular culture, including J.R.R. Tolkien's *The Lord of the Rings* and the Marvel Cinematic Universe's portrayal of Thor and Loki. These modern interpretations have helped to keep the myth relevant and influential to this day.

In conclusion, the myth of Ragnarok's influence on Norse culture and subsequent generations cannot be overstated. It provided a framework for understanding the world, emphasized the importance of bravery and sacrifice, and continues to inspire and captivate people to this day.

Modern interpretations

The myth of Ragnarok has had a significant impact on popular culture, particularly in modern times. It has been used as a source of inspiration for numerous books, movies, television shows, video games, and other forms of media.

One example of a modern interpretation of Ragnarok is Marvel Comics' *Thor* series, which features the character of Thor, based on the Norse god of thunder, as a central figure. The comics and subsequent films depict Ragnarok as a catastrophic event that threatens to destroy the entire universe, with Thor and other characters working to prevent it from happening. This interpretation has been widely popularized and has introduced the myth to a new generation of audiences.

In literature, the myth has been used as a central theme in works such as J.R.R. Tolkien's aforementioned *The Lord of the Rings* trilogy, which features an epic battle between good and evil forces, and Neil Gaiman's *American Gods*, which explores the idea of ancient gods living among modern-day humans.

In video games, the myth has been used as inspiration for various games, including *God of War*, *Final Fantasy XIV*, and *Assassin's Creed: Valhalla*, which features Viking characters and settings.

Overall, the influence of Ragnarok on modern culture is a testament to its enduring significance and relevance, even in the modern era. Its themes of destruction, rebirth, sacrifice, and the cyclical nature of life continue to resonate with people across cultures and generations.

PART 2: HARNESSING RAGNAROK FOR POSITIVE CHANGE

Harnessing the power of the myth of Ragnarok for positive change is a powerful concept. By understanding the cyclical nature of creation and destruction, we can use this myth to help us navigate change and transform ourselves and the world around us.

One example of this is the story of a man named Mark. Mark was stuck in a dead-end job that he hated, but he didn't know how to make a change. One day, he stumbled upon the myth of Ragnarok and was struck by the idea of the cyclical nature of life. He realized that his current situation was a form of destruction, but that it also presented an opportunity for new creation.

Mark decided to take action and make a change. He quit his job and went back to school to pursue a degree in a field that he was passionate about. It wasn't easy, and he had to make sacrifices along the way, but he kept the idea of Ragnarok in his mind, knowing that the destruction he faced was necessary for the creation of something new.

As he progressed through his studies, Mark began to see positive changes in his life. He was happier, more fulfilled, and more confident in his abilities. He even started a side business that allowed him to use his newfound knowledge and skills to help others.

The myth of Ragnarok helped Mark to see that change, even if it's difficult and uncomfortable, can be a positive force for transformation. By harnessing the power of this myth, he was able to turn what seemed like destruction into an opportunity for growth and new creation.

In our own lives, we can use the myth of Ragnarok to inspire us to make positive changes and transformations. This idea can give us the courage to make changes and take risks, knowing that even if we face destruction along the way, we can emerge stronger and more resilient.

We will now bring the power of Ragarok to bear on two dozen of the most painful challenges of life. Follow the instructions provided and watch your life begin to evolve in the most interesting ways imaginable. You have a bright future ahead. You just have to put in the work now to make the changes necessary to start the process.

Opening Charm

Begin each spell with this chant:

Power of fire, ice, and bone,
Ragnarok Magic now be shown.
With each strike and every blow,
Ragnarok Magic starts to flow.

End worlds, and start anew,
Ragnarok Magic, I call to you.
The cycle turns, as fate demands,

I take this power into my hands.

With every chant and every verse,
I call the power to reverse,
To change and shape what's yet to be,
Ragnarok Magic bears down on me.

Closing Charm

Conclude each spell this incantation:

I gathered the power, great and true
From Odin, Freya, and Loki too.
I unleashed the power of Ragnarok's force
And needed change has started its course.

My will is strong and my heart is brave
Ragnarok shapes the future I crave.
The old shall fade and the new shall rise
With power and wisdom, I claim my prize.

Let Odin's wisdom guide my way,
And Freya's love is here to stay.
May Loki's cunning shape my fate,
And Thor's might make me ever great.

So mote it be, my will is done
The transformation has now begun.

CHAPTER 5: ANTI-AGING

As we grow older, many of us yearn for ways to slow down or even reverse the aging process. This desire for anti-aging is natural, as we want to maintain our physical and mental faculties for as long as possible. However, the negative pain points that come with aging, such as increased physical pain, reduced mental acuity, and social isolation, can make this desire even stronger.

One of the most frustrating aspects of aging is the deterioration of our physical bodies. We may experience chronic pain, decreased mobility, and difficulty performing even simple tasks. This can limit our ability to engage in the activities we love and can even lead to feelings of isolation and depression.

In addition to physical changes, many of us also experience a decline in mental acuity as we age. We may struggle to remember things, have difficulty concentrating, and find it harder to learn new skills. This can be frustrating and even embarrassing, especially if we feel that our intelligence and abilities define us as individuals.

Despite these negative pain points, there are ways to harness the power of magic to slow down or even reverse the aging process. One such spell involves the use of a natural anti-aging ingredient such as ginseng, combined with visualization techniques to focus on reversing the effects of aging.

Waxing Moon Ragnarok Spell to Restore Youth

To begin the spell, gather a small amount of ginseng and some water in a bowl. Close your eyes and focus on the image of yourself as you were in your prime. Visualize yourself as youthful, vibrant, and full of energy. See yourself engaging in the activities you love, surrounded by friends and loved ones.

Now, take the ginseng and rub it gently onto your skin, focusing on the areas that show the most signs of aging. As you do this, repeat the following incantation:

By the power of the earth and sky,
By the wisdom of the ages gone by,
I call upon the magic of youth and life,
To restore my body and banish strife.

With this ginseng, I call forth the power,
To reverse the ravages of time's dark hour,
To feel the energy and vitality of youth,
And live with joy and passion, in love and truth.

Repeat this incantation 9 times, visualizing the youthful image of yourself growing stronger and clearer in your mind's eye. As you do this, feel the power of the earth and sky flowing through you, revitalizing your body and mind.

When you are finished, rinse off the ginseng and water and dry your skin. Take a few moments to relax and center yourself, feeling the renewed energy and vitality flowing through you. With this spell, you can harness the power of magic to slow down or even reverse the aging process, allowing you to live with joy and passion, in love and truth.

Repeat this spell as often as once a day on a Sunday, Monday, Thursday, or Friday during the waxing moon until you feel it taking effect.

Waning Moon Ragnarok Spell to Decrease Effects of Aging

In addition, you may use this alternative spell during the waning moon to reduce the effect of aging.

To reduce the effects of aging, use the Elder Futhark rune Uruz, which represents the healing power of nature. This spell should be done during the waning moon on a Tuesday, Wednesday, or Saturday, when the moon is decreasing in size, to symbolize the slowing down of aging. You may do it as often as once a day or night.

To perform this spell, you will need a small piece of paper or parchment, a pen or marker, and an Uruz rune written in red ink on white paper:

ᚾ

Light a white candle and focus your mind on the intention of reducing the effects of aging.

Hold the rune in your hand and recite the following chant:

By the power of Uruz,
I'm an aging wine.
As the moon wanes,
My years decline.
By the power of Freya,
My pain is reduced
Forgetfulness flees
I'm no longer confused.

Visualize yourself feeling less pain and less mental constraints as the effects of aging are diminished. When you feel ready, blow out the candle and carry the Uruz rune with you as a talisman to continue the spell's effects. Repeat this spell on a Tuesday, Wednesday, or Saturday, during the waning moon phase as needed to maintain its potency.

CHAPTER 6: REDUCE STRESS

Stress is a very real and potent force that can have a negative impact on our physical, mental, and spiritual well-being. In our modern world, stress is a constant companion, and its effects can be debilitating. Chronic stress can lead to physical ailments such as high blood pressure, heart disease, and depression. It can also impact our cognitive function, leading to forgetfulness, lack of concentration, and poor decision-making skills.

I once knew a woman who was under so much stress that she nearly lost her mind. She was a working mother with three children, a demanding job, and a spouse who was often absent. She was overwhelmed by the responsibilities of her life and felt as though she was drowning in a sea of obligations. She found it difficult to focus on anything, and her thoughts were constantly scattered. She was anxious and depressed, and she felt as though she was slowly losing her grip on reality.

However, with the help of magic, she was able to find some relief. She learned a spell that helped her to clear her mind and reduce her stress levels. The spell involved burning a candle and reciting a simple incantation. She would sit in a quiet room, light the candle, and focus on the flame while reciting the incantation. Within a few minutes, she would feel her stress melting away, and her mind would become clear and focused.

This simple spell helped the woman to regain control of her life. She was able to focus on her work and her family without feeling overwhelmed, and she was able to find moments of peace and relaxation throughout the day. The stress that had once threatened to consume her was now under her control, and she was able to live a happier and healthier life.

In conclusion, stress is a very real and potent force that can have negative impacts on our lives. However, with the help of magic, we can reduce our stress levels and find moments of peace and relaxation. The spell I have shared is just one example of the many ways in which magic can help us to improve our lives and find greater balance and harmony.

Here is this spell that uses candle magic to eliminate stress:

Ragnarok Spell to Reduce Stress

Ingredients:
- One white candle
- One blue candle
- Lavender essential oil
- A small bowl of water

Instructions:
1. Find a quiet place where you won't be disturbed and set up your materials.

2. Take a few deep breaths and clear your mind.

3. Anoint the white candle with lavender oil, starting at the top and moving down to the bottom.

4. Anoint the blue candle with lavender oil, starting at the bottom and moving up to the top.

5. Light the white candle and say: "I light this candle to bring peace and calmness into my life."

6. Light the blue candle and say: "I light this candle to release stress and tension from my body and mind."

7. Take a few deep breaths and focus on the flames of the candles.

8. Imagine the stress and tension leaving your body and mind and being absorbed into the flames of the blue candle.

9. With the story of death and rebirth from the Ragnarok myth in your mind, look into the candlelight of the white candle and repeat this incantation 9 times:

**"Fire burning bright,
Cleanse my mind and bring me light.
Let stress and worry fade away,
Bring me peace both day and night."**

10. When you feel ready, take the bowl of water and dip your fingers into it.

11. Use your wet fingers to extinguish the blue candle, saying: "As this candle goes out, so does my stress and tension."

12. Use your fingers to extinguish the white candle, saying: "As this candle goes out, I am filled with peace and calmness."

13. Dispose of the candles and water in a safe and respectful manner.

Repeat this spell as needed on each Monday, Friday and Sunday during the waxing moon.

As a boost to this spell, carry the Elhaz rune in your left pocket or purse every day to bring you a sense of spiritual protection and support from the powers on high.

Remember that spells are not a substitute for seeking professional help if you are experiencing severe or chronic stress. If you are struggling with stress or mental health issues, please reach out to a trusted healthcare provider or mental health professional for assistance.

CHAPTER 7: WEIGHT LOSS

Once there was a woman named Karen who had struggled with her weight for years. She had tried every fad diet and exercise regimen under the sun but had never been able to stick to anything long enough to see results. Karen had resigned herself to a life of being overweight and unhappy.

One day, Karen was walking through the park and saw a butterfly emerging from its cocoon. She watched in amazement as the butterfly struggled to free itself from its confines, eventually breaking free and spreading its wings. Karen was struck by the beauty of the butterfly and realized that it was a symbol of new beginnings and transformation.

Inspired by the butterfly's journey, Karen decided to make a change. She started by taking small steps, like cutting back on sugary drinks and taking short walks each day. As she began to see results, Karen became more motivated to continue her journey.

With time, Karen lost weight and regained her confidence. She felt like a new person, free from the weight that had held her back for so long. Karen realized that new beginnings were possible, and that she had the power to transform her life.

The story of Karen shows that new beginnings are possible, no matter how difficult or impossible they may seem at first. Just like the butterfly emerging from its cocoon, we too can break free from our confines and transform ourselves into something new and beautiful. All it takes is the courage to take that first step and the determination to keep going, even when the journey gets tough.

Ragnarok Rune Spell for Weight Loss

I shall provide you with a rune spell ritual for weight loss, utilizing the power of Uruz, the rune of life, vitality, energy, health, and connection to the world of nature. This ritual is a sacred act of harnessing the runic forces to support your journey towards a healthier body.

Begin by finding a quiet and serene space where you can be undisturbed. Place an Uruz rune symbol, carved or drawn, in front of you. Light a green or white candle, symbolizing the energy of life and health. Take a few deep breaths, centering yourself in the present moment.

ᚾ

As you gaze upon the Uruz rune, envision your body becoming strong and vibrant, filled with vital energy. Feel a deep connection with the primal forces of nature, tapping into the power of the rune. Allow this energy to flow through you, revitalizing every cell and supporting your weight loss goals.

70

Recite the following chant:

**"Uruz, rune of strength and vitality,
Guide me on this path of transformation,
Grant me the power to shed what no longer
serves,
And embrace a body in harmony with nature's
flow."**

Feel the energy of the Uruz rune merging with your intentions. Visualize excess weight melting away, replaced by a healthier, more balanced body. Hold this vision in your mind's eye and feel the determination to make positive choices in your daily life.

Take a moment to express gratitude to the rune and the forces it represents. Blow out the candle, symbolizing the release of your intention into the universe. Carry the Uruz symbol with you or place it in a sacred space as a reminder of your commitment to your well-being.

Remember, this spell is a tool to support your weight loss journey, but it must be complemented by healthy lifestyle choices and self-care practices. Use the energy and guidance of Uruz to stay motivated, make conscious dietary decisions, and engage in regular physical activity.

May the power of Uruz be with you on your path to a healthier and more vibrant life. So mote it be.

CHAPTER 8: ACCELERATED LEARNING

Let's dive into the fascinating topic of accelerated learning—its benefits, methods, and potential dangers. Accelerated learning is the pursuit of acquiring knowledge and skills in an efficient and effective manner, allowing individuals to grasp information quickly and retain it for long-term use. It's like turbocharging your brain!

The benefits of accelerated learning are tremendous. By mastering the techniques of efficient learning, individuals can save valuable time, absorb information faster, and enhance their overall productivity. Whether it's mastering a new language, acquiring technical skills, or staying updated in a rapidly changing world, accelerated learning gives you a competitive edge.

One popular method for accelerated learning is known as "chunking." This involves breaking down complex subjects into smaller, manageable chunks, making them easier to comprehend and remember. By organizing information in a logical and structured manner, learners can process it more effectively.

Another technique is "spaced repetition," which involves reviewing information at strategic intervals. Instead of cramming all the material at once, spaced repetition allows for regular review sessions, reinforcing memory and promoting long-term retention.

However, it's essential to be aware of the potential dangers of accelerated learning. The pursuit of rapid knowledge acquisition can sometimes lead to a shallow understanding of a subject. While accelerated learning can be a powerful tool, it's crucial to strike a balance between speed and depth. Taking the time to explore concepts thoroughly and engage in critical thinking is vital for a comprehensive understanding.

Additionally, it's important to avoid overwhelming oneself with excessive information. In our information-driven age, it's easy to fall into the trap of "information overload." To avoid this, focus on quality over quantity, select reliable sources, and prioritize the most relevant and useful information for your goals.

Remember, the key to successful accelerated learning lies in finding the right balance and combining various techniques that work best for you. Experiment, adapt, and refine your approach based on your unique learning style and preferences.

So, seize the power of accelerated learning, and watch your knowledge and skills soar to new heights. With dedication, effective strategies, and a curious mindset, you can become a learning machine, constantly expanding your horizons and embracing new opportunities. Get ready to unlock your potential and conquer the world of knowledge!

Ragnarok Rune Spell for Accelerated Learning

Let me guide you through a spell for accelerated learning, drawing upon the powerful energies of the Kenaz rune. The Kenaz rune represents the transformative power of fire, igniting your intellect, creativity, and the swift acquisition of knowledge. Prepare yourself for a journey of enhanced learning and wisdom.

To begin, find a quiet and peaceful space where you can focus your energy. Light a red or orange candle, representing the vibrant flames of knowledge and inspiration. Place it before you, and gaze into the flickering light as it dances with life.

Take a deep breath, center yourself, and recite the following incantation:

**"By the sacred fires that burn within,
I call upon the rune of Kenaz to begin.
Ignite my mind, let knowledge flow,
Accelerate my learning, so mote it be, I know."**

Feel the warmth and energy of the flame enveloping you, awakening your inner fire. Visualize a brilliant light emanating from the candle, infusing your mind with clarity and focus. Envision the Kenaz rune glowing brightly, its power merging with your own.

Now, with a sense of purpose, state your intention clearly and confidently:

74

**"With each new study and every page turned,
May the energies of Kenaz be learned.
Grant me the swiftness of comprehension,
Accelerated learning in my possession."**

As you utter these words, imagine a golden aura enveloping you, symbolizing the accelerated flow of knowledge and understanding. Visualize the subjects you wish to learn, envisioning yourself effortlessly absorbing information and retaining it with ease.

To conclude the spell, express your gratitude to the energies of the Kenaz rune:

**"Kenaz, I thank you for your guiding light,
Empowering me to learn with all my might.
May your fire burn within me forevermore,
Accelerated learning, my spirit shall soar."**

Allow the candle to burn for a while as a symbol of your commitment to accelerated learning. Whenever you engage in studying or learning activities, light the same candle, invoking the energy of Kenaz to support your efforts.

Remember, the power of accelerated learning lies within you, and with the aid of the Kenaz rune, you can tap into your innate abilities to acquire knowledge swiftly and passionately. Embrace the fire within, let it fuel your curiosity, and watch as your learning potential expands and flourishes.

CHAPTER 9: BEAUTY

Ah, the pursuit of beauty, a noble aspiration indeed! Freya is the Goddess of Beauty. Let us turn to her for some guidance in this imaginary conversation.

ME: Freya, Goddess of Beauty, I desire to increase my relationship with beauty. What would you suggest I do?

FREYA: To enhance your relationship with beauty, consider the following suggestions:

1. Appreciate Nature's Beauty: Spend time in nature, observing its wonders. Marvel at the delicate petals of flowers, the soothing sound of a babbling brook, or the grandeur of a majestic sunset. Nature holds boundless beauty waiting to be discovered.

2. Cultivate Inner Beauty: True beauty radiates from within. Nourish your mind, body, and spirit through self-care practices such as meditation, exercise, and pursuing activities that bring you joy. A balanced and harmonious inner self will enhance your outer beauty.

3. Surround Yourself with Beauty: Fill your living spaces with elements that bring you joy and delight your senses. Decorate your surroundings with art, flowers, and objects that resonate with your aesthetic preferences. Beauty in your environment can uplift your spirit.

4. Express Yourself Creatively: Engage in artistic pursuits that allow you to express your unique vision of beauty. Paint, write, dance, or engage in any form of creative expression that resonates with your soul. Unleashing your creativity is a beautiful way to connect with the essence of beauty.

5. Cultivate Gratitude: Be grateful for the beauty that already exists in your life. Practice gratitude for the simple pleasures, the moments of awe, and the connections you have with others. Gratitude opens your eyes to the beauty that surrounds you.

Remember, beauty is a personal and subjective experience. Embrace what resonates with your own sense of aesthetics and let it guide you on your journey. May the pursuit of beauty bring you joy and fulfillment!

ME: What is it about you, Freya, that makes you so beautiful, other than your gorgeous body?

FREYA: As the Goddess of beauty, it is said that my allure extends beyond just my physical appearance. While physical beauty can be captivating, true beauty is multi-faceted and encompasses various aspects. Here are some qualities that contribute to the beauty associated with Freya:

1. Inner Radiance: Beauty starts from within. It is the light that shines through a person's soul, reflecting their kindness, compassion, and love. It is the way one treats others and

carries oneself with grace and integrity.

2. Confidence and Empowerment: Beauty is also found in the confidence to be oneself, embracing individuality and uniqueness. It is the power to express one's thoughts, desires, and emotions authentically. Confidence is captivating and adds a magnetic charm to one's presence.

3. Love and Passion: Love is a beautiful and transformative force. As the Goddess of love, I embody the ability to love deeply and passionately, and to inspire love in others. Love can radiate through our actions, relationships, and the way we connect with the world around us.

4. Wisdom and Knowledge: True beauty is often accompanied by wisdom and intellect. The pursuit of knowledge, the ability to understand and empathize, and the wisdom gained from life experiences can add depth and allure to one's beauty.

5. Vitality and Joy: Beauty is also reflected in vitality and a zest for life. It is the ability to find joy in both the small and grand moments, embracing the present with enthusiasm and a positive outlook. Radiating joy can be captivating and infectious.

These qualities contribute to the overall beauty associated with Freya, extending beyond the external appearance. Remember, beauty is subjective and can manifest in diverse ways.

Embrace your own unique qualities and let your inner beauty shine.

ME: Thank you, Freya! You are brilliant. I love you.

FREYA: Oh, how delightful to hear such words! As the Goddess of love, I cherish your affection and appreciation. I send you my warmest regards and love in return. May your journey be filled with beauty, love, and joy. If you ever require guidance or simply wish to connect again, know that I am here for you.

Ragnarok Rune Spell for Beauty

Here is a rune spell utilizing the Gebo rune to enhance your beauty. Here is a simple rune spell for you:

Find a quiet and comfortable space where you can focus your energy.

Hold a piece of paper or parchment in your hands. Visualize the Gebo rune, with its arms and legs wide open, symbolizing the welcoming embrace of beauty and love.

X

Take a moment to connect with your intention and desire to enhance your beauty. Feel the warmth of good feelings and self-love within you.

79

With a pen or marker, draw the Gebo rune on the paper. As you do so, visualize your beauty expanding and radiating from within you, spreading its enchanting energy to the world around you.

While focusing on the Gebo rune, recite the following affirmation or your own personalized words:

**"By the power of Gebo's embrace,
I call forth beauty and grace.
Within me, it shall reside,
Radiating out, far and wide.
From heart to face, to every part,
I embrace beauty in my art.
As I will, so mote it be."**

Visualize the energy of the Gebo rune infused into the paper, carrying your intention for increased beauty.

Fold the paper and keep it in a safe place, such as a special box or your bedside table. You can also carry it with you as a reminder of your beauty and the intention you have set.

Remember, this rune spell is a symbolic representation of your intention and desire. It is important to complement it with self-care practices, positive affirmations, and actions that align with your pursuit of beauty. Embrace your inner and outer beauty, and let it shine brightly for all to see.

CHAPTER 10: SELF-HYPNOSIS

Self-hypnosis is a powerful tool that can unlock the hidden potential of our minds and transform our lives. It is a technique that allows individuals to induce a state of focused relaxation, where the subconscious mind becomes more receptive to positive suggestions and change. The practice of self-hypnosis has gained popularity due to its numerous benefits and its ability to tap into our own inner resources for personal growth and improvement.

One of the key powers of self-hypnosis lies in its ability to harness the immense power of our subconscious mind. Our subconscious mind holds deep-rooted beliefs, patterns, and habits that shape our thoughts, behaviors, and experiences. By entering a state of deep relaxation and accessing the subconscious, self-hypnosis enables us to reprogram these beliefs and patterns, replacing them with more empowering and positive ones.

Self-hypnosis can be used for a wide range of purposes, from overcoming fears and phobias to improving self-confidence, managing stress, and enhancing performance in various areas of life. Through focused visualization and suggestion, we can cultivate a heightened state of awareness, sharpen our focus, and strengthen our resilience.

Furthermore, self-hypnosis serves as a valuable tool for relaxation and stress reduction. By inducing a state of deep relaxation, it helps to calm the mind, release tension, and promote overall well-being. Regular practice of self-hypnosis can lead to improved sleep, increased focus, and a greater sense of inner peace and tranquility.

It is important to note that self-hypnosis is a skill that requires practice and consistency. Like any other practice, the more we engage in it, the more proficient we become. Learning and mastering self-hypnosis can empower us to take charge of our own personal development and unleash our full potential.

Ragnarok Rune Spell for Self-Hypnosis

Incorporating the power of the Laguz rune, we can create a simple yet effective rune spell for self-hypnosis. This spell will help us tap into the depths of our unconscious mind and plant seeds of positive change. Remember, all things are possible when we harness the energy within.

To begin, find a quiet and comfortable space where you can relax and focus. Take a few deep breaths, allowing yourself to release any tension or distractions.

Next, visualize a calm and serene lake, representing your deep unconscious mind. See the gentle ripples and feel the peaceful energy emanating from the water.

Hold the Laguz rune in your hand, connecting with its energy. Feel its power and association with the depths of your unconscious mind.

ᛚ

Recite the following incantation:

"Laguz, thou rune of the deep unknown,
Guide me to my unconscious throne.
I sail upon your tranquil lake,
To harness power for my own sake.

Within the depths, my mind does roam,
Planting thoughts that I will own.
I shape my thoughts, my conscious guide,
All things are possible, with you by my side.

Laguz, unlock the hidden door,
Allow my conscious mind to soar.
Implant thoughts of success and gain,
As I journey within, my power I'll retain."

Hold the rune to your heart, visualizing the energy of the Laguz rune infusing your being. Feel a sense of empowerment and connection with your deep unconscious mind.

Allow yourself to remain in this state for a few moments, absorbing the energy and affirming your ability to achieve your desires.

When you are ready, slowly bring yourself back to the present moment. Take a deep breath and express gratitude for the power of self-hypnosis and the potential it holds for personal transformation.

Remember, as you embark on your self-hypnosis journey, embrace the belief that all things are possible. Trust in the power of your unconscious mind and the ability to shape your thoughts, behaviors, and outcomes.

So mote it be.

CHAPTER 11: BETTER GRADES

Making better grades is a crucial aspect of academic success. It is a reflection of one's dedication, effort, and ability to grasp and apply knowledge. While grades are not the sole measure of intelligence or capability, they play a significant role in unlocking opportunities and achieving future goals.

Consider the story of a young man named Alex, who found himself struggling with his grades during his first year of college. He had always been a diligent student in high school, but the transition to a new academic environment proved to be challenging. Alex's grades suffered, and he began to doubt his abilities and future prospects.

One day, while researching different study techniques, Alex stumbled upon a book on magical practices. Intrigued, he delved into the subject and discovered the concept of using magic to enhance his learning abilities and improve his grades.

With a blend of skepticism and curiosity, Alex decided to give it a try. He created a personal ritual, incorporating visualization techniques and the use of symbolic objects to represent his academic goals. Each night before studying, he would light a candle and focus his mind on his desired outcomes, visualizing himself understanding complex concepts and excelling in exams.

To his surprise, Alex noticed a significant

shift in his learning experience. He found himself more focused, retaining information with ease, and feeling a sense of confidence and clarity during exams. It was as if his connection to the magical practice had unlocked a hidden potential within him.

Over time, Alex's grades began to improve steadily. His professors noticed his increased engagement and the quality of his work. He felt a renewed sense of purpose and drive, fueled by his newfound study techniques and the belief that he had the power to shape his academic destiny.

Through his dedication and the unconventional use of magic, Alex transformed his academic performance. The challenges he initially faced became stepping stones to his success. With each improved grade, he gained not only a sense of accomplishment but also a growing belief in his abilities.

The story of Alex illustrates the challenges many students face and the transformative power of belief and determination. While magic may not be a conventional solution, it serves as a metaphor for the importance of mindset and finding personalized strategies to overcome obstacles.

Better grades are crucial to success because they open doors to future opportunities. They demonstrate not only mastery of a subject but also qualities such as discipline, perseverance, and a commitment to personal growth. Improved grades can lead to scholarships, internships, job offers, and a solid foundation for future endeavors.

In the journey toward better grades, it is essential to explore various techniques, embrace a growth mindset, and leverage one's unique strengths. Like Alex, we can draw inspiration from unconventional sources, blending imagination with practical strategies, and ultimately realizing our full potential.

Remember, success is not solely determined by grades, but they can serve as a powerful indicator of your dedication and ability to achieve your goals. Embrace the challenges, tap into your inner resources, and believe in your capacity to make remarkable progress. The path to better grades is within your reach, and with the right mindset, dedication, and perhaps a touch of magic, you can unlock your true academic potential.

Ragnarok Rune Spell for Better Grades

Here is a rune spell to enhance your learning process and improve your grades. The rune we will work with is Raidho, representing the journey and the path we take towards our goals.

To begin, find a quiet and comfortable space where you can focus your attention. Take a few deep breaths to center yourself and clear your mind. Hold a piece of paper or an object with the symbol of Raidho, or simply visualize the rune in your mind's eye.

Repeat the following chant, allowing the words to resonate within you:

**"By the power of Raidho's sacred might,
A journey to improve my learning and insight.
Like a carriage on a well-planned path,
I navigate my studies, overcoming any aftermath.**

**With each step I take, knowledge unfolds,
Understanding deepens, my mind becomes bold.
I embrace the process, I embrace the way,
Finding methods that work, day by day.**

**I release distractions, I sharpen my focus,
With Raidho's guidance, my learning is the locus.
I adapt and refine, discovering what's best,
Creating a journey that leads to success.**

**By Raidho's energy, I strive to excel,
Improving my grades, I cast my spell.
With determination, effort, and wisdom, I align,
Unlocking my potential, one grade at a time.**

So mote it be."

Visualize yourself confidently engaged in your studies, absorbing information effortlessly, and achieving your desired grades. Feel the energy of Raidho supporting your journey and guiding you towards success.

After reciting the chant, express gratitude for the guidance and power of Raidho. Keep the symbol or object with you as a reminder of your commitment to your learning journey.

Remember, this spell is a tool to enhance your learning process, but it is essential to couple it with dedicated effort, effective study techniques, and a growth mindset. Let Raidho inspire you to embrace the path of continuous learning and improvement, unlocking your true academic potential.

May the power of Raidho guide you on your journey to better grades and a brighter future.

CHAPTER 12: PERSONALITY POWER

Now let's delve into the concept of personality power and its significance in our lives. Personality power refers to the ability to leverage our unique qualities, traits, and behaviors to influence and shape our interactions, opportunities, and overall success.

One's personality is like a toolbox, filled with a variety of tools that can be utilized to navigate through life's challenges and achieve desired outcomes. It's not just about having a charismatic or outgoing personality; it's about understanding and utilizing the strengths and qualities that make us who we are.

First and foremost, personality power is crucial because it allows us to build and maintain positive relationships. By understanding our own personality traits and those of others, we can communicate effectively, empathize, and connect on a deeper level. This interpersonal skill is invaluable in both personal and professional settings, as it fosters collaboration, teamwork, and mutual respect.

Furthermore, personality power enables us to influence and persuade others. Whether it's in negotiations, presentations, or everyday interactions, our unique blend of communication style, confidence, and charisma can make a significant impact. By leveraging our strengths and adapting to different situations, we can inspire, motivate, and shape the outcomes we desire.

Another aspect of personality power is self-confidence and self-belief. When we embrace and showcase our authentic selves, it instills a sense of confidence and attracts opportunities. People are naturally drawn to those who exude self-assurance and authenticity. By embracing our quirks, talents, and passions, we can create a magnetic presence that opens doors and paves the way for success.

However, it's important to recognize that personality power is not about being manipulative or inauthentic. It's about understanding ourselves, embracing our strengths, and continuously growing and evolving. It's about being self-aware and harnessing our unique qualities to make a positive impact on ourselves and others.

Ultimately, personality power is a tool that can help us navigate the complexities of life, influence our surroundings, and achieve our goals. It's a lifelong journey of self-discovery and personal development. By embracing our personality power and leveraging it wisely, we can unlock our full potential and create a life that aligns with our authentic selves.

Remember, it's not about changing who you are, but about embracing and amplifying the best version of yourself. So go forth, embrace your personality power, and let it guide you to success in all aspects of life.

Ragnarok Rune Spell for Personality Power using the Ansuz Rune

This rune spell will unlock your personality power, drawing inspiration from the mighty rune Ansuz, associated with persuasion, personality, and power. By channeling the energy of Odin, the master of wisdom and influence, you can tap into your own charismatic potential and unleash the hidden benefits within.

Find a quiet and comfortable space where you can focus your energy and intentions without distractions.

Set up an altar or sacred space adorned with symbols that resonate with you, such as a representation of Odin or a depiction of the Ansuz rune.

Light a candle to symbolize the flame of your personality power, illuminating your path to persuasion.

Take a few deep breaths, centering yourself and connecting with your inner self.

Hold a rune stone or draw the Ansuz rune on a piece of paper, focusing your attention on it.

Recite the following chant, feeling the energy and essence of Ansuz flowing through you:

"By the power of Odin's might,

I awaken my personality's light.
Ansuz, guide me with your persuasive sway,
Unleash my charisma in every way."

Visualize yourself radiating confidence, charm, and persuasive energy. Imagine people being drawn to your presence and captivated by your words.

Repeat the chant three times, allowing the energy to build and fill your being with the essence of Ansuz.

Thank Odin for his guidance and power, expressing gratitude for the newfound personality power that will manifest in your life.

Close the ritual by extinguishing the candle, symbolizing the integration of the energy into your being.

Remember, the true power of this rune spell lies within you. As you go about your days, embrace the qualities of persuasion, charisma, and personal power. Allow the energy of Ansuz to guide your interactions and influence those around you in positive and meaningful ways.

With practice and the ongoing exploration of your personality power, you will discover the secret benefits that come from tapping into this potent force. Embrace the essence of Ansuz and watch as your persuasive abilities grow, opening doors and creating opportunities in both personal and professional realms.

Harness the rune of Ansuz, embody the

charisma of Odin, and let your personality power shine brightly. The world awaits your influential presence and the positive impact you will make.

Ragnarok Rune Spell for Personality Power using Wunjo

Here's a rune spell for you using Wunjo as the rune to increase your personality power:

Find a quiet and comfortable space where you can focus your energy.

Hold a piece of paper or parchment in your hands. Visualize the Wunjo rune, its shape representing the celebration and connection with like-minded individuals.

Take a moment to connect with your intention and desire to enhance your personality power. Feel the sense of connection and confidence growing within you, as if you were celebrating with kin and kindred spirits.

With a pen or marker, draw the Wunjo rune on the paper. As you do so, imagine your personality blossoming and shining brightly, as if in the midst of a joyous celebration.

While focusing on the Wunjo rune, recite the following affirmation or adapt it to your own words:

**"With Wunjo's power, my personality awakes,
A celebration of connections it makes.
Confidence and openness now arise,
Communicating with ease, no disguise.
Like-minded souls, we come together,
Sharing joys and creating a bond forever.
As I will, so mote it be."**

Visualize the energy of the Wunjo rune infusing the paper, carrying your intention for enhanced personality power and communication skills.

Fold the paper and keep it in a safe place, such as a special box or your pocket. Carry it with you as a reminder of your intention and the celebration of connection you seek.

Remember, this rune spell is a symbolic representation of your intention and desire. It is important to complement it with actions and practices that align with enhancing your communication skills and building connections. Embrace the sense of celebration and openness in your interactions with others.

CHAPTER 13: MEMORY

Once upon a time, in a quiet suburban neighborhood, lived a middle-aged woman named Cindy. Cindy had always been content with her life, but as the years passed, she began to feel a sense of restlessness and longing for something more. She yearned for a deeper connection to herself and a renewed sense of purpose.

One day, while cleaning out the attic, Cindy stumbled upon a box filled with old photo albums, letters, and memorabilia from her youth. As she flipped through the faded photographs and read the heartfelt letters, a flood of memories came rushing back to her. It was as if a door to her past had swung open, revealing a world she had long forgotten.

In that moment, Cindy realized the transformative power of memory. She saw how her past experiences had shaped her into the person she was today, and she recognized the valuable lessons hidden within those forgotten moments. Inspired by this newfound realization, Cindy embarked on a journey of self-discovery, using the power of memory as her guiding compass.

She started journaling, documenting her memories, thoughts, and reflections. Each day, she would sit with a cup of tea, flipping through the pages of her journals and allowing the memories to resurface. She reconnected with old friends, revisited places she had once loved, and engaged in activities that sparked nostalgia and joy.

As Cindy delved deeper into her memories, she began to see patterns and themes emerging. She discovered a passion for art that had been buried for years, and she enrolled in painting classes to reawaken her creativity. She also found solace in revisiting cherished childhood hobbies, such as gardening and playing the piano, reigniting a sense of playfulness and wonder that had long been dormant.

The transformative power of memory not only revitalized Cindy's spirit but also brought a renewed sense of purpose to her life. She became more present in her interactions with others, drawing upon the wisdom and experiences gained from her past. Her relationships blossomed as she shared stories, memories, and lessons with her loved ones, deepening their connections and creating a sense of shared history.

Cindy's newfound appreciation for memory also helped her navigate life's challenges with grace and resilience. When faced with difficult decisions or moments of uncertainty, she would draw strength from the memories of past triumphs and the lessons learned from past mistakes. She found that by tapping into the reservoir of her experiences, she possessed a wellspring of knowledge and intuition to guide her forward.

In the end, Cindy's journey of self-discovery and the transformative power of memory allowed her to reclaim her authentic self and live a life filled with purpose, joy, and fulfillment. She became a living testament to the idea that our memories hold within them the seeds of personal growth, transformation, and a deeper understanding of ourselves.

And so, as Cindy continued on her journey, she embraced the power of memory, treasuring each moment and weaving her past into the tapestry of her present. Through the transformative lens of memory, she discovered the true essence of who she was and unlocked the limitless potential for a brighter, more meaningful future.

Let's discuss the power of memory and its profound impact on personal transformation and the pursuit of power. Memory serves as the foundation upon which our abilities, knowledge, and experiences are built. It is the gateway to unlocking our true potential and achieving greatness.

The ability to recall information, experiences, and lessons from the past provides us with a powerful tool for personal growth and development. It allows us to learn from our mistakes, make informed decisions, and adapt to new challenges. By leveraging the power of memory, we can tap into a vast reservoir of knowledge and wisdom that propels us forward on our journey to success.

Memory also plays a crucial role in shaping our identity and sense of self. Our memories form the fabric of our personal narratives, influencing our beliefs, values, and behaviors. By consciously selecting and reinforcing positive memories, we can shape our mindset and build a strong foundation for personal power. The memories we choose to hold onto and draw strength from become the building blocks of our confidence, resilience, and determination.

By revisiting past experiences and memories, we can reframe them in a way that empowers us. We can reinterpret challenges as opportunities for growth, extract valuable lessons from setbacks, and identify patterns that hinder our progress.

To harness the power of memory, it is important to adopt effective memory techniques and practices. These may include techniques such as visualization, repetition, association, and storytelling. By consciously engaging with our memories and actively working to strengthen our recollection abilities, we enhance our cognitive powers and expand our capacity for learning, problem-solving, and creative thinking.

In conclusion, memory is a fundamental pillar of personal power and transformation. It forms the bedrock of our knowledge, skills, and experiences, and provides us with the tools to navigate life's challenges and seize opportunities. By embracing the power of memory, we can tap into our true potential, shape our identity, and embark on a transformative journey toward success. So, remember to remember, for within the depths of memory lie the keys to unlocking your power and achieving greatness.

Ragnarok Rune Spell for Memory with Tiwaz

Find a quiet and comfortable space where you can focus your energy.

Hold a piece of paper or parchment in your hands. Visualize the Tiwaz rune, representing the victory and sacrifice of Tyr for the benefit of his people.

Take a moment to connect with your intention and desire to increase memory, overcoming forgetfulness, and achieving victory over memory loss.

With a pen or marker, draw the Tiwaz rune on the paper. As you do so, imagine the rune imbued with the power of Tyr's sacrifice, symbolizing victory and mental clarity.

While focusing on the Tiwaz rune, recite the following affirmation or adapt it to your own words:

**"By the power of Tiwaz, victory I claim,
Over memory loss, I rise to acclaim.
Like Tyr's sacrifice, my mind shall prevail,
Clear and sharp, memory shall not fail.
Past and present, knowledge shall be retained,
Victory over forgetfulness, I have gained.
As I will, so mote it be."**

Visualize the energy of the Tiwaz rune infusing the paper, carrying your intention for improved memory and mental clarity.

Fold the paper and keep it in a safe place, such as a special box or your study area. You may also carry it with you as a reminder of your intention and the victory over memory loss you seek.

Remember, this rune spell is a symbolic representation of your intention and desire. It is important to complement it with practices that support memory enhancement, such as mental exercises, a healthy lifestyle, and maintaining an organized and stimulating environment.

CHAPTER 14: BACK PAIN

Back pain, a common affliction that affects millions of people, can be a debilitating condition that hinders one's ability to live a normal, pain-free life. It can be caused by various factors, such as muscle strain, poor posture, herniated discs, or even underlying medical conditions. The pain can range from mild discomfort to severe agony, making it difficult to perform daily activities or find relief.

Finding a cure for back pain can be a complex and individualized process. It often involves a combination of approaches, including physical therapy, exercise, medication, lifestyle modifications, and sometimes even surgical intervention. Each person's journey to finding relief may differ, as the causes and severity of back pain vary greatly from person to person.

Here is a story of one gentleman whose back pain cure included the use of rune magic.

Magic Success Story: An Older Man's Magic Cures His Back Pain

In a small town nestled amidst rolling hills, there lived an old man named Harold. For years, he had suffered from chronic back pain that made each day a struggle. The pain restricted his movements, preventing him from enjoying simple pleasures like walking in the park or playing with his grandchildren.

Despite trying various treatments and therapies, Harold's pain persisted, leaving him frustrated and disheartened. However, deep within him, Harold held a belief in the power of magic and the ability to harness unseen forces for healing.

One day, while sitting in his study surrounded by books on folklore and ancient rituals, Harold stumbled upon an old grimoire that contained a spell for relieving pain. The spell focused on the rune Elhaz, known for its protective and healing properties. Eager to find a solution, Harold decided to give it a try.

With great determination, Harold set up a small altar in his bedroom, adorned with candles, herbs, and symbols of healing. He recited the incantation from the grimoire, calling upon the energies of Elhaz to alleviate his back pain and restore his mobility.

Days turned into weeks, and Harold continued his magical practice, combining it with daily stretches and gentle exercises recommended by his physical therapist. Slowly but surely, he began to notice a remarkable improvement in his condition. The pain that had plagued him for years started to fade, replaced by a newfound sense of comfort and vitality.

As the months passed, Harold's back pain became a distant memory. He reveled in the joy of taking long walks, tending to his garden, and even playing catch with his grandchildren. The transformation was nothing short of magical, a testament to the power of belief, perseverance, and a touch of mysticism.

Word of Harold's remarkable recovery spread through the town, inspiring others who suffered from chronic pain to explore alternative avenues for healing. His success story became a beacon of hope, reminding everyone that even in the face of adversity, there are hidden forces at play, waiting to be tapped into and harnessed.

And so, Harold's journey to overcome back pain through the power of magic not only transformed his own life but also touched the lives of those around him. His story serves as a reminder that sometimes, the answers we seek are found in the realms beyond the tangible, and that with an open mind and a dash of enchantment, miracles can unfold even in the most unexpected of ways.

Here is a rune spell similar to the one Harold used.

Ragnarok Rune Spell for Back Pain with Elhaz

This is a rune spell for the cure of back pain, harnessing the transformative energies of the Elhaz rune, a symbol of healing and protection. This spell is designed to invite the healing spirits to infuse their golden light into the affected area, bringing relief and restoration.

Prepare yourself for the spell by finding a quiet space where you can be undisturbed. Gather a white candle, a small cloth pouch, and a piece of paper with the Elhaz rune drawn upon it.

Light the white candle, allowing its pure flame to fill the space with warmth and light.

Hold the piece of paper with the Elhaz rune in your hand and close your eyes. Visualize a radiant golden light surrounding you, infusing you with healing energy.

Recite the following incantation:

"Ancient spirits of healing grace,
I call upon you in this sacred space.
Elhaz, bring forth your golden light,
Banish pain and restore with all your might."

Place the paper with the Elhaz rune inside the cloth pouch, symbolizing the containment of healing energy.

Hold the pouch against the affected area of your back, allowing the rune's power to penetrate and soothe the pain. Visualize the golden light of the healing spirits infusing the area, dissolving tension and discomfort.

Take a few moments to breathe deeply and relax, feeling the healing energy spreading throughout your body.

Express your gratitude to the spirits and the Elhaz rune for their assistance in your healing journey.

Snuff out the candle, signaling the end of the spell.

Carry the cloth pouch with you as a reminder of the healing energy you have invoked. Whenever you experience back pain, hold the pouch against the affected area and visualize the golden light of the healing spirits bringing relief and restoration.

Remember, this rune spell is intended as a complementary approach to healing. It is important to consult with healthcare professionals for a comprehensive treatment plan for your back pain. The power of the Elhaz rune, combined with modern medicine and holistic practices, can bring about transformative healing and well-being.

CHAPTER 15: MAKE MORE MONEY

Everyone needs more money. It's a fact of life that financial security and abundance provide us with opportunities, peace of mind, and the ability to pursue our dreams. Take the story of a young married couple who found themselves struggling with a lack of money. Their bills piled up, debts loomed, and they even contemplated applying for public housing just to make ends meet. They were at their lowest point, feeling defeated and trapped in a cycle of scarcity.

But then, they stumbled upon the power of rune magic. They discovered that the runes held not only ancient wisdom but also the potential to manifest their desires. With newfound hope, they embarked on a journey to invoke the energies of abundance and prosperity into their lives.

Using the runes, they crafted a spell focused on drawing in more money and financial stability. With faith and intention, they incorporated the power of Fehu, the rune of wealth and abundance, into their daily practices. They visualized their bank account growing, opportunities flowing in, and their financial worries dissipating.

Miraculously, their efforts began to bear fruit. Unexpected opportunities for advancement and financial gain appeared. They secured new sources of income, and their debts gradually diminished. They no longer needed to rely on public housing but instead found themselves living in a comfortable home they could call their own. The power of rune magic had lifted them out of their despair and propelled them towards a life of abundance and prosperity.

With the right mindset, strategic use of runes, and a belief in the possibilities that lie ahead, we too can unlock the doors to financial abundance and create a brighter future.

Ragnarok Rune Spell for Making More Money with Fehu

Here's a rune spell utilizing the energy of Fehu to help attract more money into your life:

Find a quiet and comfortable space where you can focus your intention. Place a candle on a table or altar, representing the fire energy of transformation and manifestation.

Take a deep breath and center yourself. Hold a small piece of paper or parchment in your hands, and with a pen or marker, draw the Fehu rune. Visualize this rune glowing with a golden light, symbolizing wealth and abundance.

As you hold the rune, repeat the following affirmation:

"By the power of Fehu, the rune of prosperity, I call upon the energies of abundance and

prosperity.
Like the cattle multiply and thrive,
So shall my financial resources grow and
thrive."

Envision your desired financial situation. Imagine money flowing to you effortlessly, opportunities for financial gain, and a secure and prosperous future. Feel the excitement and gratitude as if these desires have already been fulfilled.

Place the paper with the Fehu rune under your candle. Light the candle, allowing the flame to represent the transformative power of your intention.

Let the candle burn down completely, symbolizing the ongoing energy and manifestation of abundance in your life. As the candle burns, hold the vision of financial prosperity and repeat your affirmation.

Once the candle has burned out, collect the remains and bury them in the earth, symbolizing the grounding of your intentions and the integration of abundance into your life.

Remember, the power of this spell lies in your belief, intention, and consistent action. Keep your focus on abundance, remain open to opportunities, and take inspired steps towards your financial goals. The Fehu rune serves as a powerful symbol and catalyst for attracting and multiplying your wealth.

CHAPTER 16: STOP SMOKING

Smoking cigarettes poses significant dangers to both your immediate and long-term health. The harmful effects of smoking are well-documented, and they can impact nearly every organ and system in your body. On the other hand, quitting smoking can have numerous benefits for your health and overall well-being.

Remember, quitting smoking is a challenging process, but with determination, support, and resources available, it is possible to overcome this addiction and improve your health and well-being.

Ragnarok Rune Spell for Stopping Smoking

I present to you a powerful rune spell to aid you in your quest to quit smoking and embrace a healthier lifestyle. The Uruz rune, symbolizing health, vitality, and the formidable strength of a wild bull, will serve as the foundation of this spell.

Find a quiet and comfortable space where you can focus your energy.

Draw the Uruz symbol on a small piece of paper.

Light a white candle to symbolize purity and

the burning away of negative influences.

Take a few deep breaths, allowing yourself to relax and center your mind.

Hold the paper with the Uruz symbol in your hands.

Close your eyes and visualize the fierce strength of a wild bull flowing through you.

Speak the following incantation with conviction and determination:

"By the might of Uruz, I call upon the ancient force,
To break the chains of smoking, to reclaim my health's course.
Like a wild bull's power, I stand firm and resolute,
Breaking free from this habit, my vitality is absolute."

Repeat the affirmation aloud or in your mind, infusing it with your intention:

"I am free from smoking, my body vibrant and strong,
With the force of Uruz, I choose health all lifelong.
The determination of the wild bull fuels my will,
Smoking no longer controls me, I am free to fulfill."

Visualize yourself as a vibrant, healthy individual, no longer dependent on smoking. See yourself enjoying a life of vitality and well-being.

Offer gratitude to the Uruz rune and the ancient wild bull energy for their assistance.

Blow out the candle, symbolizing the end of the ritual.

Remember, this rune spell is a powerful tool to support your journey, but it is essential to complement it with your determination and commitment to quit smoking. Use this spell as a catalyst for change and embrace the vitality and strength that Uruz represents. May the force of the ancient wild bull guide you on your path to a smoke-free and healthier life.

CHAPTER 17: ARTHRITIS

Once upon a time, in a small town nestled amidst rolling hills, there lived an older woman named Eleanor. She had lived a vibrant life, but in her later years, she found herself plagued by the relentless grip of arthritis. The pain in her joints was a constant companion, limiting her movements and dampening her spirits.

Eleanor had tried countless remedies, from conventional medications to alternative therapies, but nothing seemed to provide lasting relief. Frustrated and weary, she began to lose hope, until one fateful day, a book opened her eyes to the power of rune magic.

Intrigued by the mystical symbols, Eleanor delved into the world of runes, seeking answers to her persistent agony. She discovered that the Uruz rune, with its representation of strength and vitality, held the potential to alleviate her suffering. With renewed determination, she embarked on a journey to harness the power of Uruz and find relief from her arthritis.

Eleanor diligently studied the ancient wisdom associated with the Uruz rune. She learned of its ability to restore energy and vitality to the body, to heal and strengthen weary joints. With newfound hope, she incorporated Uruz into her daily routine, using it as a focal point for her intentions.

Every morning, Eleanor would sit in a quiet

corner of her home, holding an Uruz rune stone in her hands. She closed her eyes, envisioning a vibrant green light surrounding her, permeating her joints with revitalizing energy. With each breath, she chanted affirmations of strength and healing, directing the power of Uruz towards her arthritic pain.

Days turned into weeks, and weeks into months. Gradually, Eleanor began to notice subtle changes in her body. The intensity of her arthritis pain lessened, allowing her to move more freely and engage in activities she had once thought impossible. Her spirit rekindled, and a renewed sense of vitality coursed through her veins.

With each passing day, Eleanor's connection with Uruz grew stronger. She learned to listen to her body, to nurture it with care and compassion. The Uruz rune became her symbol of resilience and perseverance, a reminder of the strength within her to overcome adversity.

Word of Eleanor's remarkable transformation spread throughout the town, and soon others with arthritis sought her guidance. She shared her knowledge of Uruz and guided them on their own paths to healing. Eleanor's journey of pain and discovery had not only transformed her life but also became a beacon of hope for others in need.

From that day forward, Eleanor became known as the wise woman who had tamed the fiery pain of arthritis with the power of Uruz. She continued to inspire others, reminding them that within the ancient wisdom of runes lies the potential for transformation and healing.

And so, Eleanor's story serves as a testament to the incredible power of belief, perseverance, and the magic of Uruz. May her journey continue to inspire those who seek relief from physical ailments and remind us all that sometimes, the greatest remedies lie within the depths of our own spirits.

Ragnarok Rune Spell for Arthritis Relief

Uruz is the rune associated with strength, vitality, and physical well-being. Here is an updated version of the rune spell for healing arthritis using Uruz:

Find a quiet and comfortable space where you can focus your energy.

Obtain an Uruz rune stone or draw the Uruz symbol on a small piece of paper.

ᚾ

Light a green candle to symbolize healing and renewal.

Take a few deep breaths, allowing yourself to relax and center your mind.

Hold the Uruz rune stone or paper with the Uruz symbol in your hands. Close your eyes and imagine a vibrant green light surrounding you, infusing you with strength and vitality.

Speak the following incantation with sincerity and clarity:

"With Uruz's mighty force, I call upon its strength,
To heal my joints, restore my body's health at length.
Vitality and resilience flow through every part,
Arthritis dissipates, replaced with a renewed start."

Repeat the affirmation aloud or in your mind, infusing it with your intention:

"Arthritis fades away, my body is restored,
Uruz's healing power, I gratefully afford.
Joints regain their flexibility, pain dissolves and departs,
I embrace vibrant health, a renewed lease on life starts."

Feel strong and healthy in your joints. See yourself engaging in activities with ease and joy.

Express gratitude to the power of Uruz and the healing energy it represents.

Blow out the candle.

Remember to incorporate this rune spell as a complementary practice alongside proper medical care, lifestyle adjustments, and any prescribed treatments for arthritis. May the energy of Uruz support your healing journey and contribute to your overall well-being.

CHAPTER 18: BECOMING POPULAR AND LIKED

In the bustling halls of Brookside High School, there lived a young man named Alex. He was a quiet and introspective soul, always on the outskirts of social circles, never quite fitting in. Alex longed for companionship and acceptance, but his timid nature and lack of confidence seemed to repel those around him.

Day after day, Alex endured the taunts and teasing from his classmates, feeling like an outsider in his own world. But deep within him, there was a flicker of hope, a desire to break free from the chains of isolation and forge meaningful connections.

Intrigued, he began to delve into the world of runes, seeking solace and understanding in these enigmatic symbols. Among them, he discovered the Ehwaz rune, with its vision of a horse and rider, symbolizing partnership and cooperation.

Inspired by the power and symbolism of Ehwaz, Alex embarked on a transformative journey to overcome his social obstacles. He spent hours studying the ways of the rune, understanding its essence and how it could bring about the changes he desired. With each passing day, Alex's connection with Ehwaz grew stronger, and he harnessed its power to reshape his high school experience.

Armed with newfound confidence, Alex ventured into the hallways of Brookside High with a renewed sense of purpose. He began to see his peers not as adversaries but as potential friends and allies. Drawing upon the energy of Ehwaz, he approached others with kindness, openness, and a genuine desire to connect.

Remarkably, the change was palpable. Classmates began to notice Alex's transformation, captivated by his newfound charisma and genuine interest in their lives. With the guidance of Ehwaz, Alex formed unexpected friendships, finding companionship and support in the unlikeliest of places.

As days turned into weeks and weeks into months, Alex's social circle expanded, and his once lonely existence transformed into a vibrant tapestry of friendships. The power of Ehwaz became a beacon of light, guiding him towards genuine connections and teaching him the value of collaboration and partnership.

Years later, as Alex reflected upon his high school days, he realized that the true power of Ehwaz lay not just in popularity but in the lessons it had taught him. Through the rune's guidance, he had learned the importance of authenticity, empathy, and the transformative power of forging genuine connections with others.

And so, the tale of Alex and the Ehwaz rune serves as a reminder that sometimes, the key to finding acceptance lies not in changing who we are but in embracing our true selves and seeking partnership with those who appreciate us for who we are. May we all be inspired by Alex's journey and the power of Ehwaz to transform our own lives and bring about a sense of belonging and connection.

Ragnarok Rune Spell for using Ehwaz to bring Partnership, Friendship and Help

Begin by creating a calm and sacred atmosphere in your chosen space. Light a white or blue candle and allow its gentle glow to fill the room, creating a soothing ambiance.

Take a piece of paper and a black marker or pen. On the paper, draw the Ehwaz rune with focused intent and clarity. As you draw each line, visualize the vision of a horse and rider, symbolizing partnership, friendship, and the support you seek.

Hold the paper with both hands and close your eyes. Take a few deep breaths to center yourself and connect with the energy of Ehwaz. Feel its power flowing through your being, awakening a sense of connection and unity.

With utmost sincerity, speak the following incantation:

**Ehwaz, rune of partnership and friendship,
I call upon your ancient power and grace.
In the spirit of Ragnarok, I seek your aid,
To bring forth allies, bonds, and support in my
life's embrace.
Let the energy of Ehwaz guide me on this quest,
Manifesting partnerships and friendships that
are blessed.
By the forces of Asgard, I summon this aid,
So mote it be!**

Place the paper with the Ehwaz rune in a safe spot, close to the lit candle. Allow the flame to infuse the symbol with the energy of transformation and manifestation.

Sit quietly for a few moments, visualizing the desired outcomes of partnership, friendship, and help entering your life. See yourself surrounded by supportive and loyal companions who uplift and assist you on your journey.

Once you feel ready, extinguish the candle and give thanks to Ehwaz for its guidance and assistance. Trust that the energies set in motion by the spell will unfold in their own perfect time.

Keep the paper with the Ehwaz rune in a sacred space or carry it with you as a reminder of your intentions. You may choose to revisit the spell, recharge it, or modify it as needed in your journey to attract and nurture meaningful partnerships and friendships.

CHAPTER 19: YOGA

Yoga as a spiritual practice has profound physical health benefits. Yoga has gained popularity worldwide for its ability to harmonize the mind, body, and spirit, creating a holistic approach to well-being.

First and foremost, yoga is a powerful tool for cultivating inner peace and tranquility. Through its various practices, such as asanas (physical postures), pranayama (breathing exercises), and meditation, yoga helps individuals connect with their inner selves, promoting a sense of calm and mental clarity. It offers a sanctuary from the chaotic demands of modern life, allowing practitioners to find solace and balance amidst the daily hustle and bustle.

Beyond the spiritual aspects, yoga also offers a multitude of physical health benefits. The practice of asanas improves flexibility, strength, and balance, enhancing overall body fitness. The deliberate and mindful movements in yoga postures gently stretch and tone muscles, promoting better posture and alignment. This can help alleviate chronic pain and improve joint mobility.

Moreover, yoga is renowned for its stress-reducing effects. By incorporating conscious breathing techniques and meditation, yoga helps activate the body's relaxation response, reducing stress hormones and inducing a deep sense of relaxation. This can have a positive impact on cardiovascular health, lower blood pressure, and improve immune function.

Yoga is not merely an exercise regimen; it is a transformative practice that goes beyond the physical realm. It encourages self-reflection, self-acceptance, and self-compassion, fostering a deeper understanding of oneself and others. Through regular practice, individuals can cultivate mindfulness, emotional resilience, and a greater sense of connection to the world around them.

Sarah's Story

Let me share with you the profound impact of combining the Ingwaz rune with the practice of yoga to deepen one's spiritual experience and enhance the connection with the cosmos.

Imagine a young businesswoman named Sarah who, despite her outward success, felt a deep longing for something more meaningful in her life. Seeking solace and inner growth, she turned to yoga as a way to find balance and tap into her inner wisdom. It was during this journey that she discovered the power of the Ingwaz rune, which resonated deeply with her.

Sarah understood the Ingwaz rune as a symbol of hidden potential, secret growth, and the concept of biding time. Inspired by this vision of a seed, she began incorporating the Ingwaz rune into her yoga practice. She would meditate on the rune, visualizing herself as the seed, rooted in the earth and connected to the cosmic energy above.

As Sarah practiced yoga, she focused on nurturing her body and mind, allowing the energy to flow freely within her. The combination of yoga and the Ingwaz rune acted as a catalyst for her spiritual growth. She felt a profound sense of connection with the universe, as if she was tapping into the hidden potential within herself and the world around her.

During her yoga sessions, Sarah experienced moments of deep introspection and self-awareness. The practice allowed her to quiet the noise of her busy life and tune in to the subtle energies within her own body. She felt a heightened sense of intuition, as if the universe was guiding her towards her true purpose.

Over time, Sarah noticed a remarkable transformation taking place. She became more attuned to her body's needs, listening to its whispers and responding with care. The integration of the Ingwaz rune into her practice seemed to awaken a deeper connection between her body, mind, and spirit. She felt a renewed sense of vitality and clarity, as if she had unlocked a wellspring of inner wisdom.

The Ingwaz rune has the power to supercharge the spiritual effects of yoga, enhancing the connection with the cosmos and facilitating profound self-discovery. By incorporating the vision of a seed and the concept of hidden potential into the practice, individuals like Sarah can tap into their inner wisdom, deepen their spiritual experience, and find a profound connection with their own bodies and the universe at large.

Ragnarok Rune Spell to Empower Yoga with Ingwaz

You will need:

- A small piece of paper or parchment
- A pen or marker
- A quiet and sacred space

Begin by finding a calm and sacred space where you can focus your energy and intention. Light a candle or some incense to create a peaceful atmosphere.

Take a few deep breaths, allowing yourself to relax and center your mind. Visualize yourself surrounded by a radiant golden light, connecting you to the cosmic energies.

Take the piece of paper or parchment and write the Ingwaz rune symbol on it. As you draw the rune, imagine the hidden potential within you, ready to unfold and manifest.

Hold the paper in your hands and close your eyes. Visualize yourself in a yoga practice, feeling the energy flowing through your body, connecting you to the earth and the cosmos.

Repeat the following incantation aloud or in your mind:

"Ingwaz rune, I call upon your power,
Unleash the hidden potential within,
Empower my yoga practice with divine energy,
Connect me to the cosmic realm where wisdom resides.
As I flow through poses, I embrace my growth,
Nurturing body, mind, and soul,
Ingwaz, guide me on this sacred journey,
Awaken the seeds of transformation within me."

Place the paper or parchment with the Ingwaz rune symbol in a sacred space or carry it with you during your yoga practice. Allow its presence to remind you of your intention to connect with the hidden potential and wisdom within.

Conclude the ritual by expressing gratitude for the energy of the Ingwaz rune and the divine guidance it brings to your yoga practice. Blow out the candle or let the incense burn out naturally.

CHAPTER 20: READING PEOPLE

Reading people, the art of understanding and interpreting non-verbal cues and behavioral patterns, is a powerful skill that can bring numerous benefits in various aspects of life. By honing this ability, we can gain valuable insights into the thoughts, feelings, and intentions of others, enhancing our communication, relationships, and decision-making. Let's explore some of the benefits of reading people.

Firstly, being adept at reading people allows us to build stronger connections and rapport. We can better understand the emotions and needs of those around us, fostering empathy and creating a sense of trust. This skill enables us to tailor our communication style and approach, leading to more effective interactions and improved relationships.

Secondly, the ability to read people can enhance our leadership skills. By recognizing the dynamics within a group or team, we can adapt our leadership style accordingly, empowering individuals and fostering a collaborative and harmonious environment. Understanding the strengths and weaknesses of team members helps in assigning tasks and delegating responsibilities more efficiently, leading to increased productivity and success.

Furthermore, reading people can aid in making better decisions. By observing non-verbal cues, facial expressions, and body language, we can gauge the authenticity of a person's words and intentions. This skill can be particularly useful in negotiations, job interviews, or any situation where detecting deception or hidden motives is crucial.

Let's delve into a story of someone who mastered the art of reading people and reaped significant rewards. Meet Nicole, a sales professional who was struggling to close deals and connect with her clients effectively. Realizing the importance of understanding her clients' needs and motivations, she devoted time and effort to studying body language, microexpressions, and verbal cues.

Through diligent practice and observation, Nicole became highly skilled at reading people. She could identify when clients were genuinely interested or hesitant, whether they needed more information or reassurance, and how to adapt her sales pitch accordingly. Nicole's newfound ability to understand her clients on a deeper level allowed her to build trust, tailor her approach, and address their concerns effectively.

As a result, Nicole's sales performance skyrocketed. Her closing rates improved significantly, and she developed long-term, mutually beneficial relationships with her clients. By reading people, Sarah gained a competitive edge in her industry, earning a reputation for being attentive, empathetic, and insightful.

Ragnarok Rune Spell: Reading People with Mannaz

127

Ingredients:

- A Mannaz rune or image
- A quiet and comfortable space
- Focus and intention

Begin by finding a quiet space where you can relax and focus without distractions. Create an atmosphere that promotes calmness and concentration.

Hold the Mannaz rune or image in your hands and take a few deep breaths. Close your eyes and visualize the image of the crowned human, representing the evolution, consciousness, and perfection within yourself.

Repeat the following incantation, speaking it aloud or silently:

"By the power of Mannaz, the rune of evolution, I seek the wisdom to understand and perceive. Grant me the insight to read the hearts and minds of others, Unveiling the hidden truths they seek to weave."

Visualize the energy of the Mannaz rune flowing into your being, awakening your consciousness and intuition. Feel the crown upon your head symbolizing your heightened awareness and understanding.

Open your eyes and bring your attention to the people you wish to read. Observe their body language, facial expressions, and subtle cues. Trust your instincts and intuition to guide you in interpreting their thoughts, emotions, and intentions.

Take note of any insights or impressions that come to you. Pay attention to your own feelings and sensations as you interact with others, as they can provide valuable clues and insights.

After your interactions, take time to reflect on what you have observed and learned. Use this newfound knowledge to enhance your understanding of others, improve your communication skills, and deepen your connections.

Express gratitude to Mannaz and the cosmic forces for their guidance and assistance in your quest to read people.

Remember, reading people is a skill that requires practice, patience, and ongoing refinement. Keep honing your abilities by observing and interacting with others, and trust in the power of Mannaz to enhance your understanding of human nature and the intricate tapestry of thoughts and emotions we all carry. May your journey of reading people bring you wisdom, compassion, and meaningful connections.

CHAPTER 21: HOW TO BE A BETTER WORKING MOTHER

Being a working mother is a balancing act that comes with its own set of challenges. Juggling the responsibilities of work and family can often leave mothers feeling overwhelmed, stressed, and torn between their personal and professional lives. However, with the power of the Othala rune, working mothers can find strength, stability, and a sense of belonging in both realms. Let us explore the challenges faced by working mothers and how the Othala rune can help them become better, empowered mothers.

One of the primary challenges for working mothers is finding a balance between their career aspirations and their desire to be present for their children. The Othala rune, represented by the vision of a homestead, reminds working mothers of the importance of creating a firm foundation for their families. By establishing routines, boundaries, and clear communication, mothers can create a stable and nurturing home environment that supports both their work commitments and their children's needs.

Another challenge is the constant juggling of time and energy. Working mothers often find themselves stretched thin, trying to meet the demands of their careers while still being available for their children. The Othala rune reminds mothers to prioritize self-care and self-nurturing. By taking care of their own well-being, working mothers can replenish their energy reserves and be more present and engaged with their children.

Furthermore, the Othala rune embodies the concept of belonging and enduring wealth. It reminds working mothers that their efforts contribute to the prosperity and security of their families. By embracing the power of Othala, working mothers can cultivate a sense of pride and accomplishment in their professional pursuits while nurturing their family's well-being.

Ragnarok Rune Spell for Empowered Working Mothers: Harnessing the Power of Othala

Components:

- A candle representing stability and abundance
- A small dish of soil or seeds symbolizing growth and nurturing
- A piece of paper and a pen

Find a quiet and comfortable space where you can focus without distractions. Light the candle, allowing its warm glow to fill the room.

Take a few deep breaths, centering yourself in the present moment. Visualize a nurturing homestead, a place of love, stability, and prosperity.

Take the piece of paper and write down your intentions as a working mother. Be specific about the aspects of your life you wish to enhance. For example, "I am a confident and capable working

131

mother. I create a harmonious balance between my career and family. I provide a nurturing and supportive home environment."

Hold the piece of paper in your hands and close your eyes. Envision the energy of Othala, the vision of the homestead, surrounding you. Feel a sense of belonging, strength, and abundance flowing through you.

Place the piece of paper in the dish of soil or seeds, symbolizing the foundation upon which you will build your empowered journey as a working mother. Visualize the seeds of your intentions taking root, growing into a flourishing garden of balance, success, and joy.

Repeat the following incantation, speaking it with conviction and belief:

**"With Othala's might, I forge my path,
A working mother empowered in her stead,
I belong, I build, I nurture with care,
My homestead thrives, a foundation fair."**

Sit in contemplation for a few moments, basking in the energy of your intentions and the power of the Othala rune. Allow yourself to feel the connection between your aspirations as a working mother and the ancient wisdom embedded within the rune.

When you are ready, extinguish the candle,

132

knowing that the energy and intention you have set forth will continue to guide and support you on your journey.

Keep the piece of paper and the dish of soil or seeds in a special place, such as your personal altar or a sacred space, as a reminder of your commitment to being an empowered working mother.

Remember, this spell is a catalyst for change, but its true power lies in your actions and dedication to your intentions. Embrace the energy of Othala, building a firm foundation and cultivating enduring wealth in all aspects of your life as a working mother.

CHAPTER 22: MORE MALE STAMINA

So, gentlemen, let's talk about male stamina and why it matters. We all know that having more stamina can be a game-changer, not just in the bedroom, but in life as a whole. It's like having a secret superpower that allows you to go the extra mile and tackle whatever challenges come your way.

First things first, physical fitness is key. When you're in good shape, your stamina gets a boost. Regular exercise, especially cardiovascular workouts, gets your heart pumping and your blood flowing, ensuring that all the right parts of your body are well-nourished and ready to perform.

But it's not just about pumping iron and running laps. A balanced diet plays a role too. Fuel your body with nutritious foods, including lean proteins, whole grains, and plenty of fruits and vegetables. Think of it as providing your stamina engine with high-quality fuel to keep it running smoothly.

Now, let's address the elephant in the room – stress. We all know that stress can be a stamina killer. Finding effective ways to manage stress, whether it's through meditation, deep breathing exercises, or even indulging in a hobby, can work wonders for your stamina and overall well-being.

And let's not forget about the importance of a good night's sleep. Quality rest is like recharging your stamina batteries. So, make sleep a priority, create a cozy sleep environment, and aim for those recommended hours of shut-eye to wake up refreshed and ready to take on the day.

Remember, gentlemen, improving stamina is not just about physicality; it's about taking care of yourself on multiple levels. So, take charge, prioritize your health, and unleash that hidden well of stamina within you. You'll be amazed at the positive impact it can have on your life.

Ragnarok Rune Spell for More Male Stamina: Harnessing the Power of Uruz

Enjoy this powerful rune ritual harnessing the energy of Uruz to enhance male stamina. Uruz, symbolized by the mighty Wild Bull, embodies vitality, ferocity, and strength. Through this ritual, we seek to tap into these qualities and awaken the latent stamina within.

Here's what you'll need for the ritual:

1. Uruz Rune: Craft or acquire a Uruz rune symbol. It can be carved or etched on a piece of wood, or drawn on a piece of paper.

ᚾ

2. Red Candle: A candle symbolizing the fiery energy of Uruz.
3. Frankincense Incense: Frankincense is known for its energizing and invigorating

properties.
4. Sacred Space: Create a sacred space for the ritual, preferably a quiet and secluded area where you can focus without distractions.

Now, let's begin the ritual:

Light the red candle and the frankincense incense. Take a few deep breaths to center yourself and enter a calm state of mind.

Hold the Uruz rune in your hands and visualize the image of the Wild Bull, radiating with vitality and strength. Recite the following invocation:

**"By the power of Uruz, the Wild Bull's might,
I call upon the energy of stamina, day and night.
Vitality and strength, flow through my veins,
Empower my body, remove all strains."**

Repeat this invocation three times, feeling the energy building within you.

Hold the Uruz rune to your heart and affirm your intention for increased stamina. Speak aloud with conviction:

**"With the power of Uruz, I claim my stamina,
Vitality flows through me, in abundance.
I am strong, fierce, and full of might,
Stamina is my birthright, day and night."**

Visualize yourself embodying the energy of the Wild Bull, feeling invigorated and full of vitality.

Thank the energy of Uruz for its presence and assistance. Blow out the candle and let the frankincense incense continue to burn.

Remember, this ritual is a symbolic representation of your intention to enhance male stamina. It is essential to complement it with a healthy lifestyle, including regular exercise, proper nutrition, and sufficient rest. The ritual serves as a catalyst to awaken your inner strength and vitality.

May the power of Uruz guide you towards increased stamina and a vibrant sense of well-being.

CHAPTER 23: GREEN THUMB GARDENING

In a quaint little town nestled amidst rolling hills and fertile fields, there lived a woman named JoAnn. With her gentle demeanor and a deep love for the earth, JoAnn had developed an extraordinary talent for gardening. Her green thumb seemed almost magical as she cultivated thriving gardens that yielded bountiful harvests year after year.

JoAnn possessed a deep understanding of nature's rhythms and the cycles of the seasons. She knew when to sow the seeds, when to tend to the plants, and when to reap the rewards of her hard work. But there was something more to her gardening prowess – she had discovered the runic power of Jera.

Jera, symbolized by the vision of Fields at Harvest, embodied the essence of abundance and the rewards of patience and perseverance. JoAnn would often sit amidst her garden, envisioning the golden fields at harvest time, and channeling the energy of Jera into her plants.

As the seasons passed, JoAnn's garden flourished like never before. Her vegetables grew with vibrancy, boasting vibrant colors and robust flavors. Her flowers bloomed in a riot of hues, filling the air with their sweet fragrances. The townsfolk marveled at her organic farm, for it was a testament to the beauty and abundance that nature could provide.

One year, JoAnn decided to enter the county fair's gardening competition. She carefully selected her best squash, nurturing it with love and care. As she held the prized squash in her hands, she felt the energy of Jera coursing through her veins, infusing her creation with the power of abundance.

At the county fair, JoAnn's squash stood out among the rest. Its size was awe-inspiring, a testament to the power of nature and JoAnn's green thumb. The judges couldn't help but crown it the winner of the 'Biggest Squash' award, earning JoAnn well-deserved recognition for her dedication and expertise.

JoAnn's reputation as a remarkable gardener spread far and wide, attracting visitors who sought to witness her magic firsthand. She became a beloved figure in her community, sharing her knowledge and experiences with others who yearned to unlock the secrets of bountiful harvests.

But for JoAnn, it was never just about the accolades or the recognition. It was the connection she forged with the earth, the dance of energy between her and nature, that brought her true fulfillment. Each day, she continued to tend to her garden, guided by the wisdom of Jera, and reaping the rewards of her hard work and passion.

JoAnn's story serves as an inspiration to us all, reminding us of the profound power that lies within the earth and the transformative abilities we possess when we align ourselves with its rhythms. Through her green thumb and the runic magic of

139

Jera, JoAnn not only nurtured her garden but also cultivated a deep sense of gratitude, abundance, and harmony in her life.

Ragnarok Rune Spell for a Green Thumb using Jera

In the verdant realm of nature's embrace, where the soil pulses with life and the air hums with energy, we delve into the sacred wisdom of the Jera rune. As the fields stand adorned with the ripened fruits of labor, we harness the power of Jera to awaken the green thumb within us and unlock the secrets of bountiful harvests. Let us gather our tools and invoke the runic forces to weave this Ragnarok Rune Spell.

Gather beneath the open sky, where the sun's golden rays caress the earth and bless our endeavors. With reverence in our hearts and the vision of Fields at Harvest in our minds, we open ourselves to the potent energies of Jera. Feel the ancient rhythms of nature coursing through your veins, connecting you to the cycles of growth, reward, and abundance.

Hold in your hands the seeds of intention, symbols of the work you have sown and the results you seek to manifest. As you gaze upon them, infuse them with the power of Jera. Visualize the fields at harvest, lush and overflowing with the fruits of your labor. See yourself tending to your garden with skill and love, nurturing each plant to its fullest potential.

Speak these words of empowerment:

"By the might of Jera, I awaken my green thumb,
In harmony with nature's flow, my garden will become.
Reward and earnings, the harvest I desire,
Manifest through my efforts, fueled by sacred fire."

As the incantation lingers in the air, envision the seeds absorbing the runic energies, awakening their dormant potential. Plant them gently into the fertile soil, knowing that the forces of Jera will guide their growth and bring forth abundant rewards.

Now, tend to your garden with diligence and care. Nurture each plant as if it were a cherished ally, offering water, sunlight, and loving attention. Invoke the spirit of Jera in your daily rituals, connecting to the cycles of growth and celebration. Embrace the sacred dance between you and nature, allowing the runic forces to amplify your green thumb and cultivate a flourishing garden.

In time, witness the transformation unfold before your eyes. Your garden will thrive with vitality, each plant thriving under your expert touch. The rewards of your labor will manifest in the form of vibrant blossoms, luscious fruits, and a profound sense of connection to the natural world.

As you embrace the power of Jera and honor the cycles of growth, may your green thumb flourish and your garden become a sanctuary of abundance and beauty. By walking this path of harmony and partnership with nature, you not only cultivate a bountiful harvest but also nourish your own soul and deepen your connection to the sacred web of life. So mote it be.

CHAPTER 24: PERCEIVING BUSINESS OPPORTUNITIES

Once upon a time, in the bustling world of business, there was a man named Bob who had an uncanny ability to overlook golden opportunities right under his nose. He had always dreamed of striking it rich and becoming a millionaire, but his lack of perception often left him scratching his head and wondering where he had gone wrong.

One fateful day, as Bob was sipping his morning coffee and scrolling through his Twitter feed, his eyes widened with disbelief. There, in his feed, was an article about a groundbreaking invention that had the potential to revolutionize the industry. He clicked the link to the article which mentioned that investors were flocking to get a piece of the action, and the project was estimated to be worth a staggering hundred million dollars.

Little did Bob know, the universe was teasing him with the power of the runes Fehu and Nauthiz, symbols of wealth and necessity. If only he had recognized their influence and tapped into their energy, his fortunes might have taken a drastic turn.

But alas, Bob's lack of perception was his Achilles' heel. Instead of recognizing the business opportunity for what it was, he skimmed over the article, dismissing it as just another piece of news. His mind was preoccupied with mundane tasks and worries, leaving no room for the seeds of prosperity to take root.

Months later, as the groundbreaking invention began to gain traction and capture the market, Bob found himself kicking himself for not seeing the potential when it was right in front of him. The once-in-a-lifetime opportunity had slipped through his fingers, leaving him with a feeling of regret and a longing for what could have been.

The tale of Bob serves as a humorous reminder of the importance of perceiving business opportunities in the ever-changing landscape of commerce. Had he been attuned to the power of the runes Fehu and Nauthiz, his perspective might have shifted, allowing him to see beyond the surface and seize the chance to amass a fortune.

So, dear readers, let us learn from Bob's misadventure and embrace the wisdom of the runes. May we cultivate the ability to perceive hidden opportunities, to recognize the signs of potential, and to harness the energies of wealth and necessity. In doing so, we may find ourselves on a path paved with abundance, where even the most unlikely ventures can lead to extraordinary success.

Ragnarok Spell for Perception of Business Opportunities using Fehu and Nauthiz

Listen up, folks! I've got a spell for you that'll boost your business perception to the next level. It's a fusion of two powerful runes: Fehu, representing wealth and financial prowess, and Nauthiz, symbolizing hard work and necessity. When you combine these bad boys, you'll be like a business opportunity spotting machine, raking in the cash like nobody's business!

First things first, grab a piece of paper and draw the symbols of Fehu and Nauthiz. Let those lines intertwine like a masterful dance, symbolizing the marriage of money and hard work. Put some heart and soul into it, infusing the symbols with your burning desire to see those hidden opportunities and snag yourself a fortune.

ᚠ ᚾ

Now, set the scene for your ritual. Light a candle, representing the bright light of awareness, and let its flame dance and flicker. Take a moment to clear your mind, get into the zone, and prepare yourself for some serious business mojo.

Close your eyes and visualize a whole new world unfolding before you. It's a land of untapped opportunities, obscured by the distractions of everyday life. Picture yourself stepping into this realm, feeling the weight of wealth and necessity on your shoulders. You're locked and loaded, ready to spot those hidden gems that others overlook.

Now, it's time to call upon the power of the runes. Say their names with conviction, let their vibrations fill the air, and make sure you really mean it. First, give a shout-out to Fehu, summoning its energy of abundance and financial success.

145

Then, unleash the spirit of Nauthiz, channeling its vibe of hard work and never-give-up attitude. You're harnessing the forces of the business universe, my friends!

As the energy builds up, open your eyes and take a good look at the symbol you've created. Feel its power coursing through your veins, sharpening your perception like a finely-tuned business radar. Breathe in the essence of Fehu and Nauthiz, letting their magic infuse your very being.

Now, armed with your enhanced perception, it's time to hit the streets and conquer the business world. Keep your eyes peeled for signs and signals that others might miss. Trust your gut, because those runes have given you the gift of discernment. You've got the power to seize those golden opportunities that align with your goals and aspirations.

Remember, though, it's not just about spotting opportunities, it's about having the smarts to know which ones to pursue. With Fehu and Nauthiz on your side, you've got the edge to make the right moves and build your empire.

So get out there, my friends, and let the forces of Fehu and Nauthiz guide you to the money and success you deserve. Your business perception is now dialed up to eleven, and those hidden opportunities won't stand a chance. It's time to make your mark and bring home the bacon!

Go forth, conquer, and may the runes be with you!

CHAPTER 25: GET OUT OF DEBT

Alright, folks, listen up! Today I'm going to spill the beans on how to get yourself out of debt and back on the road to financial freedom. Debt can feel like a heavy burden, but with the right mindset and a solid plan, you can break free and start living that debt-free life you've always dreamed of. So let's dive right in!

The first thing you need to do is face your debt head-on. Sit down, gather all your financial statements, and get a clear picture of what you owe. It's time to confront the numbers, my friends, and truly understand the extent of your debt. It might not be pretty, but knowledge is power, and it's the first step towards taking control.

Now that you know the extent of your debt, it's time to tighten those financial belts. Take a hard look at your expenses and identify areas where you can cut back. Maybe it's time to say goodbye to that daily gourmet coffee or put a temporary halt on your online shopping sprees. Every penny counts when you're trying to dig yourself out of debt, so be ruthless and trim the excess.

Getting out of debt requires a strategy, my friends. Start by prioritizing your debts and creating a repayment plan. Consider focusing on high-interest debts first, as they tend to be the real culprits that keep you trapped in the debt cycle. Explore options like consolidating your debts or negotiating lower interest rates. The key here is to have a clear plan of attack and stick to it.

Sometimes cutting expenses just isn't enough, and that's when it's time to get creative and boost your income. Consider taking on a side hustle, freelancing, or selling unused items. Every extra dollar you can bring in will go straight towards chipping away at that debt mountain. Remember, the goal is to get out of debt as quickly as possible, so think outside the box and find ways to increase your earnings.

If you're feeling overwhelmed or unsure of where to start, don't be afraid to seek professional guidance. Financial advisors or credit counseling services can provide valuable insights and help you navigate the murky waters of debt. They can assist in creating a tailored plan based on your specific situation, ensuring you stay on track and make informed decisions.

Getting out of debt is a journey, and it's essential to stay motivated along the way. Celebrate small victories, track your progress, and visualize the debt-free life you're working towards. Keep your eye on the prize, my friends, and remember that every step you take brings you closer to financial freedom.

So there you have it, a roadmap to help you escape the clutches of debt. It won't be easy, but with determination, discipline, and a pinch of smart financial planning, you can make it happen. Start today, take control of your financial future, and say goodbye to debt for good. You've got this!

Ragnarok Rune Spell for Getting Out of Debt using Fehu and Othala

For an extra boost from the realm of rune magic, let us harness the powers of Fehu and Othala to create a powerful spell for escaping the clutches of debt and inviting financial abundance into our lives. These runes, when combined, can ignite the fires of change and lay a solid foundation for enduring wealth. Are you ready to embark on this transformative journey? Let's begin.

Materials needed:
- A piece of paper or parchment
- A pen or marker
- A green candle
- A small dish or holder for the candle
- Optional: herbs or incense associated with prosperity (such as cinnamon or patchouli)

Find a quiet and sacred space where you can perform this ritual undisturbed. Light the green candle and place it in the dish or holder.

Take a few deep breaths to center yourself and focus your intentions on your desire to break free from debt and manifest financial abundance.

Take the piece of paper or parchment and write down all your debts, large or small. Visualize each debt being released from its hold on you as you write. Feel a sense of liberation with each stroke of the pen.

Now, draw the Fehu rune next to each debt listed. As you do so, envision streams of golden

149

light flowing from the rune, transforming each debt into a source of wealth and abundance. See yourself rising above your financial challenges and feeling a sense of relief and empowerment.

Beneath the list of debts, draw the Othala rune. Envision this rune as a solid foundation, symbolizing the strength and stability of your financial future. See it radiating a sense of belonging and security, as if it were your own homestead, protecting you from debt and welcoming in enduring wealth.

ᛟ

Hold the paper in your hands and speak the following incantation or a variation of it, with heartfelt intent:

**"By the powers of Fehu and Othala combined,
I release myself from debt that binds.
Transforming lack into abundance and gain,
I welcome enduring wealth, free from strain.
Like the sturdy homestead, my foundation is strong,
Belonging to prosperity, where I truly belong."**

Fold the paper, sealing your intentions within it. Place it near the burning candle and let it burn safely until it turns to ash. As it burns, visualize your debts dissipating into nothingness, leaving behind only the energy of abundance and financial freedom.

Sit quietly for a few moments, basking in the glow of the candle. Feel a renewed sense of optimism and confidence in your ability to overcome financial challenges and attract prosperity into your life.

Once you are ready, extinguish the candle and safely dispose of the ashes from the burned paper. Trust that the energy of this spell is now set in motion, working to manifest your financial goals and guide you towards a debt-free future.

Remember, my friends, that rune magic is a potent tool, but it must be accompanied by practical action. Take inspired steps towards managing your finances wisely, make conscious choices, and stay committed to your goals. With the combined forces of Fehu and Othala, may you find yourself liberated from debt and embraced by the enduring wealth you deserve. So mote it be.

CHAPTER 26: LEARNING MATH

Once there was a young boy named Philip who found himself struggling with math. Numbers seemed like an impenetrable fortress, and every math class felt like a battlefield. His frustration grew as he watched his classmates effortlessly grasp concepts that eluded him. The struggle with math not only affected his academic performance but also eroded his self-confidence. Philip felt as though his potential was being held back by this mathematical hurdle.

One fateful day, as Philip was seeking help, he crossed paths with a wise teacher named Mrs. Johnson. Mrs. Johnson recognized Philip's determination and his thirst for knowledge. She knew that traditional teaching methods might not be the key to unlocking his mathematical abilities. Instead, she introduced him to the mystical world of runes.

Mrs. Johnson explained the power of the Berkano rune, which symbolized growth, nurturing, and the unfolding of potential. She encouraged Philip to visualize himself as a budding mathematician, capable of understanding and conquering the challenges of numbers. The vision of a birch forest came to Philip's mind, filled with possibilities and new life.

From that moment, Philip embarked on a journey of transformation. He started incorporating the energy of Berkano into his study routine.

Whenever he faced a difficult math problem, he would take a deep breath, close his eyes, and visualize the strength and growth associated with the rune. He embraced the belief that with perseverance and the guidance of Berkano, he could become a proficient mathematician.

Over time, Philip's understanding of math blossomed. Concepts that once seemed insurmountable became clear, and equations that once confounded him now held the promise of solutions. He began to see patterns and connections that eluded others, drawing inspiration from the vision of the birch forest that Berkano presented.

Not only did Philip's mathematical abilities improve, but his confidence soared as well. The once-daunting subject became a playground for his curiosity and exploration. He no longer saw math as a barrier but as a gateway to unlocking his intellectual potential.

As the years went by, Philip's journey with Berkano continued to bear fruit. He pursued higher levels of mathematics, excelling in his studies and earning accolades for his problem-solving skills. More importantly, he discovered the joy of unraveling the mysteries of numbers and the satisfaction of using math as a tool to navigate the world.

Ragnarok Magic Rune Spell for Learning Math with Berkano

Get yourself alone in a room. Sit in silence and close your eyes and feel your body sensations. Sit with those feelings for a few minutes. Then open your eyes and light one green candle. Green is the color of nature and the Birch Tree.

Use the Opening Charm from earlier in this book.

I embrace the essence of Berkano, the rune of nurturing and growth,
To unlock the mysteries of math, expanding knowledge's trove.
In the realm of numbers, I seek to find my place,
With the power of Berkano, I'll conquer math's embrace.

I envision a vast birch forest, alive with whispers of wisdom,
A sacred space where knowledge blooms, a sanctuary in my kingdom.
Like a tender sapling, I am open to receive,
The teachings that will help me understand and believe.

With the guidance of the Mother and Child, I embark on this quest,
To nurture my mind, to cultivate my mathematical best.
I call upon the energies of Berkano, both gentle and strong,
To guide me through equations, to where solutions belong.

As I face each problem, I am filled with patience and grace,
Like a mother teaching her child, I embrace a steady pace.
I see the patterns unfold, the connections become clear,
Berkano's wisdom whispers, dispelling every fear.

I am a student of the numbers, a seeker of profound truth,
With Berkano as my guide, I unravel math's uncanny sleuth.
I tap into the nurturing power, the growth that lies within,
And watch as my understanding expands, like the forest's endless din.

In the birch forest of knowledge, I find solace and delight,
As I learn the language of math, bringing darkness into light.
Berkano, mother of learning, I honor your sacred gift,
With your guidance, I'll conquer math, my spirits now uplifted.

So mote it be, with the power of Berkano, I decree,
I embrace the path of math, unlocking its mystery.
May the energy of nurturing and growth forever guide my way,
As I learn and excel, expanding my mind day by day.

With Berkano as my ally, I am destined to succeed,
In the realm of mathematics, I fulfill my every need.
I am a student of numbers, a bearer of Berkano's flame,
Learning math with passion, forever to proclaim.

Use the Closing Charm from earlier in this book to end this ritual.

Blow out the candle. Get up and go do something else unrelated to this. Let the magic do its work in silence, over time. Rest assured it is working without you thinking about it or focusing on it. You may repeat this Berkano ritual on each New Moon to keep it fresh.

CHAPTER 27: BETTER NUTRITION FOR BETTER HEALTH

Achieving better nutrition is a fundamental pillar of better health. It's like fueling your body with high-octane energy to optimize its performance. By making conscious choices about what we eat, we can unlock a world of vitality, resilience, and overall well-being.

One of the key principles of better nutrition is to focus on whole, unprocessed foods. Embrace a balanced diet that includes a variety of fruits, vegetables, lean proteins, whole grains, and healthy fats. These nutrient-rich foods provide the essential vitamins, minerals, and antioxidants your body needs to thrive.

Portion control is another crucial aspect of better nutrition. Pay attention to serving sizes and avoid overeating. Listen to your body's signals of hunger and fullness, and aim for moderation in all things. Remember, it's not just about what you eat, but how much you eat.

Additionally, incorporating mindful eating practices can enhance your nutritional journey. Slow down, savor each bite, and truly connect with the food you're consuming. This mindful approach allows you to tune into your body's needs and make conscious choices that support your health goals.

Another valuable tip is to stay hydrated by drinking plenty of water throughout the day. Water plays a vital role in digestion, nutrient absorption, and overall bodily functions. Make it a habit to carry a reusable water bottle and sip on water regularly.

It's important to recognize that achieving better nutrition is a journey, and small changes can make a big impact over time. Gradually incorporate healthier choices into your daily routine, and celebrate the progress you make along the way. Remember, it's about progress, not perfection.

By prioritizing better nutrition, you can unlock a wealth of benefits for your health. Increased energy, improved digestion, strengthened immune system, enhanced mental clarity, and a greater sense of well-being are just a few of the rewards waiting for you. So take the first step on this path to better nutrition and start nourishing your body for optimal health and vitality.

Ragnarok Rune Magic for Better Health and Nutrition from Elhaz, Fehu and Ansuz

The combination of the Elhaz, Fehu, and Ansuz runes can be harnessed to empower and amplify the benefits of better nutrition for improved health and well-being.

Elhaz, symbolized by the Elk, Sword, and Swan, represents defense, protection, and connection. It serves as a powerful shield, safeguarding us from harm and enhancing our resilience. When applied to the realm of nutrition, Elhaz can help fortify our bodies, protecting them from the negative effects of poor dietary choices and external factors that may compromise our health.

Fehu, associated with wealth, finance, and abundance, reminds us of the importance of nourishing ourselves with quality, nutrient-dense foods. By embracing the Fehu energy, we cultivate a mindset of abundance and prioritize investing in our health through wholesome choices. This rune encourages us to seek out foods that provide essential nutrients, vitamins, and minerals to support our overall well-being.

Ansuz, represented by the image of the God Odin, embodies communication, wisdom, and inspiration. When integrated into our nutrition practices, Ansuz encourages us to seek knowledge and understanding about food and its impact on our health. It prompts us to explore different sources of information, consult with experts, and make informed decisions about what we consume. Ansuz reminds us that the power of good nutrition lies not only in the foods themselves but also in the knowledge we acquire and apply.

To harness the combined power of these runes for better health from better nutrition, a rune spell can be crafted. Begin by creating a sacred space and invoking the presence and energy of these runes. Visualize yourself surrounded by a protective shield, like the Elk's antlers or the sharpness of a sword, guarding against harmful influences.

Hold the intention of embracing an abundant mindset and attracting nourishing foods into your life. See yourself making wise choices, selecting foods that support your vitality and well-being. Feel the connection between your body and the nourishment it receives, envisioning the energy flowing through you, revitalizing and sustaining your health.

As you conclude the ritual, express gratitude to the runes and the powers they represent for guiding you towards better nutrition and improved health. Carry this intention with you as you make daily choices about what you eat, recognizing the role these runes play in protecting and connecting you to the vital energy of nourishment.

Remember, the runes are tools that can enhance our intentions and bring about positive transformations in our lives. By combining the energies of Elhaz, Fehu, and Ansuz, we can tap into their unique qualities to support and amplify the benefits of better nutrition for our overall health and well-being.

160

CHAPTER 28: ASTROLOGY

The Mystical Art of Astrology: Unveiling the Cosmic Tapestry

Astrology, a celestial language woven into the fabric of our existence, has captivated the hearts and minds of humanity for millennia. From ancient civilizations to modern societies, the study of astrology has provided insight, guidance, and a profound connection to the cosmic forces that shape our lives. We'll delve now into the mystical world of astrology, exploring its origins, principles, and the profound wisdom it offers.

The Origins of Astrology

Astrology traces its roots back to the ancient civilizations of Mesopotamia, Egypt, and Greece. Early practitioners observed the movements of celestial bodies and recognized their influence on human affairs. They perceived a deep connection between the positions of the planets and stars and the events unfolding on Earth. Over time, astrologers developed intricate systems, charting the movements of heavenly bodies and interpreting their impact on human lives.

Astrology as a Language

Astrology speaks in a unique language, employing symbols and archetypes to convey its profound wisdom. At its core, astrology recognizes that the celestial bodies are not mere distant luminaries, but mirrors reflecting the energies and patterns that shape our lives. Through the zodiac signs, planetary placements, and aspects, astrologers decode this cosmic language, offering insights into personality traits, life events, and potential paths of growth and fulfillment.

The Power of Natal Astrology

Natal astrology, also known as birth chart astrology, focuses on the precise moment of an individual's birth and provides a blueprint of their unique cosmic makeup. The natal chart serves as a map, detailing the positions of the planets and their relationships at the time of birth. By analyzing this celestial snapshot, astrologers can discern personality traits, strengths, challenges, and potential life paths, offering invaluable guidance for self-discovery and personal growth.

Astrology and Timing

Astrology is not only concerned with personality analysis but also with timing and forecasting. Through predictive astrology, astrologers explore the movements of the planets and their interactions to anticipate future trends and events. This invaluable tool helps individuals navigate life's twists and turns, make informed decisions, and align themselves with favorable cosmic energies.

Astrology as a Spiritual Journey

Beyond its predictive and psychological aspects, astrology holds a profound spiritual dimension. It invites us to recognize our interconnectedness with the cosmos and the inherent rhythms of the universe. By aligning ourselves with the planetary energies, we can embark on a transformative journey of self-discovery, self-acceptance, and spiritual growth.

Runes and Astrology

It is certainly true that the ancient runemasters knew a lot of star lore and much of that knowledge is woven into the Eddas. However, they were completely unfamiliar with astrology as we know it in modern times. Nevertheless, given that astrology is found to be so useful by so many, we may turn our hands to it, and although the runes may not share the same native origins, their power can certainly still be accessed to increase our acuity as we strive to develop our astrological skill.

Ragnarok Rune Spell for Increased Acuity with Astrology

Ingredients:
- Ansuz rune
- Perthro rune

- Astrological chart or astrology-related item (optional)

Find a quiet and comfortable space where you can focus without distractions. Take a few deep breaths to center yourself.

Hold the Ansuz rune in your dominant hand and visualize its symbol, representing wisdom, inspiration, and persuasion. Feel its energy resonating within you, awakening your inner voice and intuitive abilities.

Next, take the Perthro rune in your other hand. Envision its image of a lot cup, symbolizing luck, chance, and calculated risk. Visualize its energy intertwining with the Ansuz rune, enhancing your ability to interpret astrological patterns and foresee meaningful connections.

If you have an astrological chart or any astrology-related item, place it in front of you. Focus your gaze upon it and allow your mind to open to the cosmic energies that surround you.

Recite the following incantation, speaking from your heart with confidence and intent:

"By the power of Ansuz and Perthro combined,

I call upon the wisdom of the celestial design.
Grant me acuity and insight, clear and true,
To read the stars and skies, their secrets to
pursue.

May my intuition be heightened and refined,
As I delve into the mysteries that the cosmos
bind.
Guide me, runes of wisdom, with your ancient
lore,
Reveal the celestial patterns and so much more.

With each celestial alignment and cosmic sign,
May my understanding deepen, both profound
and fine.
Grant me clarity of thought, inspiration, and
grace,
To interpret the stars' language, with skill and
embrace.

As I embark on this astrological quest,
May the universe bless me, granting me the
best.
By Ansuz and Perthro, I align with fate's
embrace,
For in astrology's realm, I find my rightful
place."

Close your eyes and visualize yourself
surrounded by a radiant light, filled with the
energies of Ansuz and Perthro. Feel their power
infusing your mind, expanding your perception, and
granting you heightened acuity with astrology.

Take a few moments to express your gratitude for the guidance and wisdom received. When you feel ready, slowly open your eyes and conclude the ritual.

Remember, the true power of the spell lies within you. Trust in your innate abilities, study diligently, and embrace the mysteries of the stars. Through the combined energies of Ansuz and Perthro, may your acuity with astrology grow, enriching your understanding of the celestial tapestry that weaves through our lives.

CHAPTER 29: EXERCISE

In today's fast-paced and demanding world, finding happiness can sometimes feel like an elusive goal. We search for happiness in various pursuits, from career success to material possessions. However, one of the most effective and accessible paths to happiness lies right at our fingertips – exercise.

Regular physical activity is not only beneficial for our physical health but also plays a crucial role in our overall well-being and happiness. The relationship between exercise and happiness is a powerful one, rooted in the chemical and psychological changes that occur within our bodies when we engage in physical movement.

When we exercise, our bodies release endorphins, often referred to as "feel-good" hormones. These natural chemicals interact with receptors in our brain, reducing pain and triggering a positive sensation. The release of endorphins during exercise can create a state of euphoria and a sense of well-being, often known as the "runner's high." This elevated mood can contribute to a greater sense of happiness and overall life satisfaction.

Moreover, exercise has been linked to reducing symptoms of stress, anxiety, and depression. Physical activity acts as a natural stress reliever, helping to alleviate tension and clear our minds. Engaging in exercise releases pent-up energy and promotes a state of relaxation, which can positively impact our mental well-being and contribute to a more optimistic outlook on life.

In addition to the direct chemical and psychological benefits, exercise also offers a range of indirect factors that contribute to happiness. Regular physical activity can enhance our physical appearance, boost self-confidence, and improve body image. These positive changes can have a profound impact on our overall happiness and self-esteem.

Furthermore, exercise provides an opportunity for social interaction and connection. Joining group exercise classes, participating in team sports, or simply engaging in physical activities with friends and loved ones can foster a sense of community and support, adding an additional layer of fulfillment and joy to our lives.

To fully embrace the relationship between exercise and happiness, it's important to find activities that you genuinely enjoy. Whether it's running, cycling, swimming, dancing, or practicing yoga, discovering a form of exercise that brings you pleasure and fits your lifestyle will increase your motivation to engage in regular physical activity.

Remember, it's not about striving for perfection or adhering to a strict exercise routine. Start small, set realistic goals, and gradually build up your level of activity. Consistency is key. Even short bursts of exercise throughout the day, such as taking the stairs instead of the elevator or going for a brisk walk during your lunch break, can contribute to your overall well-being and happiness.

So, if you're seeking greater happiness in your life, look no further than the power of exercise. Embrace physical activity as an essential component of your daily routine, and you'll discover a profound transformation in your mood, outlook, and overall satisfaction. Get moving, and let happiness become your constant companion on the journey of life.

Ragarok Magic Rune Spell for Exercise and Happiness using Uruz and Sowillo

Ingredients:

- A piece of paper or parchment
- A pen or marker
- Uruz rune symbol
- Sowilo rune symbol

Find a quiet and comfortable space where you can focus your energy.

Take a few deep breaths to center yourself and clear your mind.

Place the piece of paper or parchment in front of you.

Draw the Uruz rune symbol in the center of the paper, visualizing the strength and vitality of a wild bull.

ᚾ

Hold the Sowilo rune symbol in your hand and close your eyes. Visualize the radiant energy of the sun, bringing guidance, confidence, and enthusiasm.

Open your eyes and place the Sowilo rune symbol on top of the Uruz rune symbol, aligning their energies.

With the pen or marker, write the following affirmation on the paper:

**"I embrace the power within me,
As I engage in exercise, I set my spirit free.
Uruz grants me vitality and strength,
Sowilo guides me with confidence and enthusiasm at length.
Through physical movement, joy will arise,
Happiness will flourish, reaching new highs."**

Read the affirmation aloud, infusing it with your intention and belief.

Fold the paper, symbolically sealing your intention within.

Keep the folded paper in a safe place or carry it with you as a reminder of your commitment to exercise and happiness.

As you engage in physical activity, visualize the Uruz and Sowilo rune symbols, channeling their energies and allowing them to empower you.

Remember, this rune spell is a tool to enhance your exercise routine and cultivate happiness. It is essential to maintain a balanced approach to exercise and listen to your body's needs. By incorporating the energies of Uruz and Sowilo, you can tap into your inner strength, embrace vitality, and infuse your physical activities with confidence and enthusiasm. May this spell guide you on your journey toward a happier and healthier life.

CONCLUSION: THE END IS JUST THE BEGINNING

As we bring this book to a close, ladies and gentlemen, let me regale you with a tale that epitomizes the profound concept of cycles of creation and destruction. Picture, if you will, the realm of Norse mythology, where the gods and giants danced to the rhythm of these eternal cycles.

In the grand narrative of creation, we witness the demise of the colossal Ymir, a giant of unimaginable magnitude. The gods, driven by a desire for innovation and progress, did not mourn this demise but instead seized the opportunity presented by Ymir's lifeless form. They harnessed the power of destruction to fashion an entirely new world from the remnants of the old. Thus sprang forth our very existence, a world far superior to its predecessor, bustling with the harmonious cohabitation of gods and humans.

Yet, this pattern of creation and destruction finds its climax in the mesmerizing myth of Ragnarok, an epoch of unparalleled upheaval. In this cataclysmic event, the gods themselves engage in a relentless battle, their colossal powers clashing in a symphony of destruction. The world as we know it faces annihilation. But fear not, for within the throes of this devastation lies the seed of rebirth. From the ashes of the old, a new world emerges, sustained by the endurance of two intrepid humans, who shall repopulate the barren land, ushering in a fresh era of existence.

Let us now venture beyond the ancient tales and delve into the wisdom of Northern Magic, where these cycles of creation and destruction serve as a resounding reminder of our innate need for change and growth. Ragnarok, with its tumultuous narrative, becomes a symbol of personal metamorphosis, a beacon of hope and transformation. It teaches us that the demolition of the outdated, the obsolete, and the stagnant is an indispensable prerequisite for forging a new and improved version of ourselves.

Enter Emma, a captivating young woman whose journey embodies the essence of this profound concept. Emma had succumbed to the clutches of addiction, reaching rock bottom and experiencing the suffocating grip of a seemingly unbreakable cycle of destruction. However, through the enchantment of Northern Magic, she uncovered a newfound appreciation for the ebbs and flows of life's cycles.

With unwavering determination, Emma recognized the crucial significance of demolishing her former way of life, as painful and daunting as it may have been. She understood that only by embracing this chaos, by surrendering to the relentless force of destruction, could she pave the way for a remarkable renaissance of her being. Guided by the teachings of Northern Magic, Emma fearlessly relinquished her old habits and beliefs, boldly embarking on a transformative odyssey.

In her quest for self-discovery, Emma discovered an unyielding reservoir of strength and resilience. She reveled in the profound understanding that destruction is not an irreversible finale, but rather an indispensable step towards rebirth and flourishing. And so, she emerged from the shadows, a phoenix reborn from the ashes, resplendent in her newfound vitality and purpose.

Emma's story resounds with an inspiring, resolute message, reminding us all that the cycles of creation and destruction should not be shunned or feared. On the contrary, they should be embraced as the catalysts of personal transformation and growth. When we acknowledge the imperative need for change, when we muster the courage to release the shackles of the old, we open ourselves to the infinite possibilities that lie before us. With determination as our guide, we can sculpt a future brimming with boundless potential, creating a life that is not merely satisfactory but profoundly fulfilling.

Revealing the Epic Lessons of Ragnarok: A Recap of Norse Mythology's Ultimate Boss Battle

Let's recap what we've learned about Ragnarok, the mother of all boss battles in Norse mythology. We're talking about a showdown where the gods themselves go toe-to-toe, and everything we know is blown to smithereens. But don't despair, because once the dust settles, we're granted a brand-spanking-new beginning. It's like hitting the reset button on the entire universe, my friends. And you know what? That's pretty darn exciting!

Now, in the realm of Northern Magic, folks seize this cosmic upheaval as a golden opportunity for self-transformation and reaching greater spiritual heights. It's a wake-up call that shakes us out of the monotonous daily grind and reminds us that life has so much more to offer. It's a chance to shake things up, break free from the chains of mediocrity, and reach for the stars!

But let me tell you, the Norse version of the apocalypse is not for the faint of heart. It's the mother of all calamities, where everything that could possibly go wrong goes wrong. Even the heavy hitters like Odin, Thor, and that mischievous scamp Loki bite the dust. The Nine Worlds of Norse cosmology? Poof! Gone in a puff of smoke. It's like watching the ultimate disaster movie unfold before your very eyes. The scale of destruction is mind-boggling.

Yet, my friends, from the smoldering ruins emerge two brave humans, ready to start anew. It's the ultimate reboot, a fresh chapter in the cosmic saga. And let's be honest here—who doesn't love a good reboot? There's something undeniably captivating about witnessing the phoenix rise from the ashes, dust itself off, and soar to new heights.

Now, let's talk about Loki. That cheeky trickster had a hand in causing all this chaos, like a cosmic pyromaniac. It's almost as if he couldn't resist stirring the pot one last time. His mischievous actions set off a cataclysmic war between the gods and the giants, obliterating everything in its path. You have to hand it to Loki; he certainly knew how to push things to the brink. But boy, did he get his wish!

Now, here's the fascinating twist: even though everything is laid to waste, it's not the end of the story. No, my friends, it's more like a necessary step in an eternal cycle of death and rebirth. It's out with the old and in with the new, like a cosmic renovation project. And that's where Northern Magic comes into play. People who embrace the teachings of Ragnarok can learn to let go of their old patterns, shed the shackles of limiting beliefs, and step into a fresh, invigorated existence. It's like a masterclass in personal growth, my friends, with the ultimate life lesson at its core.

So, buckle up and embrace the spirit of Ragnarok! Let go of the past, leave behind what no longer serves you, and charge forward with renewed vigor and purpose. Remember, my friends, destruction can be the catalyst for extraordinary transformation. It's time to seize the day, embrace change, and script your own epic saga of rebirth and personal triumph!

Rediscovering the Relevance of Ragnarok: Unveiling the Profound Lessons for Today's World

As we have learned in this book, in the depths of ancient Norse mythology lies a narrative of cataclysmic proportions, an epic saga known as

Ragnarok. As we navigate the complexities of our modern world, it is essential to rekindle our connection to these timeless tales, drawing wisdom from the past to illuminate our present and guide our future.

Ragnarok, the ultimate battle among the gods, speaks volumes about the enduring human condition and the cyclical nature of existence. It transcends its mythical origins, echoing through the ages to offer profound insights into our contemporary reality. This tale of destruction and rebirth holds a mirror to our collective experiences, inviting us to reflect on the challenges and opportunities we face today.

One might wonder, why should we delve into ancient myths when confronted with the complexities of the 21st century? The answer lies in the universal truths embedded within these stories —truths that continue to resonate and hold relevance, irrespective of time and societal context.

At its core, Ragnarok represents the eternal struggle between order and chaos, creation and destruction. We witness the gods, the very symbols of power and authority, engaging in a fierce battle that ultimately leads to the decimation of everything they held dear. The realms crumble, heroes fall, and darkness envelops all.

But from this abyss of desolation emerges a glimmer of hope. Two humans survive, standing as beacons of resilience amidst the ruins. This enduring theme of renewal and the indomitable human spirit speaks directly to our present challenges. We find ourselves grappling with a myriad of global crises, from environmental degradation to political turmoil and social unrest. Yet, within these dark clouds, we must recognize the seeds of possibility, the potential for transformative change.

Ragnarok serves as a stark reminder that even in the face of overwhelming destruction, rebirth and rejuvenation are not only possible but inevitable. It encourages us to confront our own personal Ragnaroks, those moments of profound upheaval and uncertainty, and recognize that they are not the end but rather the catalyst for growth and renewal.

The myth's relevance extends beyond personal transformation; it echoes in the collective consciousness of society. As we witness the crumbling of old systems, institutions, and beliefs, we stand at the precipice of change. Just as the gods clashed, tearing down the old order, we too find ourselves in a period of profound societal transformation. The question is, how will we navigate this tumultuous journey?

Ragnarok teaches us the importance of unity in the face of adversity. The gods, despite their individual conflicts, unite to face a common enemy. It is a call for humanity to transcend our differences and work together towards a shared future. The challenges we face today—climate change, inequality, and technological disruption—require collective action and a renewed sense of solidarity.

Moreover, Ragnarok reminds us of the resilience of the human spirit. The surviving humans in the myth symbolize our capacity to adapt, rebuild, and create anew. In the aftermath of destruction, we have the opportunity to craft a more just, equitable, and sustainable world. It is a call to harness our collective creativity and ingenuity to forge a brighter future.

Furthermore, the myth invites us to reflect on our own personal Ragnaroks—those moments of profound upheaval, loss, and uncertainty. In an ever-changing world, we face challenges that test our resilience, shake our foundations, and leave us feeling adrift. But just as the surviving humans in Ragnarok found strength and the determination to rebuild, so too can we harness our inner resolve to overcome adversity. The myth teaches us that within the darkest moments lie the seeds of transformation and the potential for personal growth.

In the midst of our hectic lives, the myth of Ragnarok serves as a reminder to pause, reflect, and reevaluate our priorities. It encourages us to look beyond the mundane routines of our existence and seek deeper meaning and purpose. By exploring the profound themes embedded within this ancient tale, we can gain a fresh perspective on our own lives and find inspiration to embark on our own journeys of self-discovery and spiritual growth.

Lessons For Modern Life in Norse Mythology

Norse mythology is a gateway to ancient wisdom and timeless insights that continue to resonate in our modern lives. By immersing ourselves in the stories and symbolism, we unlock a deeper understanding of our own journey, the nature of the cosmos, and the tapestry of human existence. Norse mythology offers a lens through which we can explore the depths of our own psyche, contemplate the mysteries of life and death, and uncover profound truths that speak to the very core of our being.

So, my fellow seekers of truth, I encourage you to embark on your own exploration of Norse mythology. Delve into the sagas, study the runes, connect with the gods and goddesses, and allow the wisdom of this ancient tradition to illuminate your path. As you delve into the realms of Norse mythology,may you discover the transformative power of these ancient tales. Let them ignite the fires of inspiration, expand your consciousness, and guide you towards a deeper understanding of yourself and the world around you.

As you study more deeply, you will find that it is not a mere collection of stories, but a living tradition that offers practical insights and guidance for navigating the complexities of modern life. The wisdom contained within the myths can be applied to various aspects of our existence, from personal relationships to professional endeavors, from spiritual growth to ecological awareness.

By embracing the virtues and ideals embodied by the gods and heroes of Norse mythology, such as courage, wisdom, honor, and perseverance, we can shape our own lives with purpose and integrity. We can learn to overcome challenges, to stand tall in the face of adversity, and to strive for greatness in all that we do.

Furthermore, the Norse tradition reminds us of the interconnectedness of all things. It calls us to honor the natural world, to respect the cycles of nature, and to foster a harmonious relationship with the environment. Through this connection with nature, we can rediscover our own inherent divinity and experience a profound sense of interconnectedness with the web of life.

As you journey deeper into the Norse cosmology, you will uncover the power of symbolism and ritual. The runes, with their ancient wisdom and mystical energy, can become potent tools for self-reflection, divination, and manifestation. By engaging with these sacred symbols, we can tap into the archetypal energies they represent and awaken dormant aspects of ourselves.

Norse mythology also invites us to explore the mysteries of the afterlife and the concept of destiny. The realms of Valhalla and Hel, the idea of reincarnation, and the concept of Wyrd all offer insights into the cyclical nature of existence and the eternal journey of the soul. By contemplating these profound themes, we can find solace in the face of mortality, gain a deeper understanding of our life's purpose, and cultivate a sense of inner peace.

So, I invite you, my fellow seekers, to embark on this transformative journey into the realms of Norse mythology. Embrace the wisdom of the gods, delve into the depths of the myths, and allow the ancient tales to guide you towards a greater understanding of yourself and the mysteries of existence. May your exploration of Norse mythology be a profound and enriching experience, leading you to discover the enduring lessons and insights that lie within this sacred tradition.

BONUS SPELL: ODIN RITUAL FOR REBIRTH

Picture this: Odin, the legendary Norse god, also known as the "Allfather," is the ultimate model of death and rebirth. Now, you might be thinking, "Death and rebirth? Sounds kind of morbid, Jón." But bear with me for a moment.

You see, Odin is not just any God. He's the ruler of Asgard, the land of the gods. And he's not just a God of War, or Wisdom, or Poetry - although he's all of those things too. No, Odin is something much greater: a God of Transformation.

Odin is a God who has died and been reborn countless times. In fact, he sacrificed his eye to gain wisdom, and he hanged himself on the World Tree Yggdrasil for nine days and nights to gain the knowledge of the runes. But even more than that, Odin is a god who understands the cycle of life and death, and he uses that understanding to bring about change and growth.

As a model for death and rebirth, Odin shows us that in order to transform ourselves, we must be willing to let go of what we once were. We must be willing to die to our old selves, to shed our skin like a snake, and emerge anew. But just as importantly, we must be willing to embrace the unknown and to trust in the power of rebirth.

Odin reminds us that death and rebirth are not just physical processes, but spiritual ones as well. And just as Odin has been reborn again and again, so too can we be reborn, transformed, and ready to face whatever challenges lie ahead.

So, if you're feeling stuck, if you're feeling like you're in a rut and you can't seem to break free, remember Odin. Remember that death and rebirth are not the end, but the beginning of something new. Trust in the power of transformation, and embrace the unknown with open arms.

Here is a bonus ritual to help you. You will need:

- A candle
- A bowl of water
- A piece of paper and pen
- Optional: runes or other symbolic objects

Begin by lighting the candle and placing it in front of you. Take a few deep breaths and center yourself.

Hold the bowl of water and reflect on the concept of rebirth. Consider the things in your life that you would like to leave behind and the new things you would like to bring forth.

Take the piece of paper and write down the things you want to release, the things you want to let go of. Be specific and honest with yourself.

Hold the paper in your hand and focus on Odin as the model for death and rebirth. Meditate on his sacrifice, how he gave up his eye to gain greater wisdom and insight.

Visualize Odin standing before you, offering to take the paper from your hand and sacrifice it for you, burning away the old to make way for the new. Imagine yourself giving the paper to him and watch as he sets it aflame with his spear as you set it aflame with a lighter or match.

As the paper burns, hold the bowl of water in your other hand and visualize the things you want to bring forth, the things you want to manifest in your life. Focus on the positive changes you want to make and the new opportunities you want to embrace.

After the paper has burned, extinguish the candle and pour the water into the bowl of ashes. As you do so, say a few words to acknowledge the transformation you are seeking to make.

End the ritual by thanking Odin for his guidance and support in your journey of death and rebirth. Blow out the candle and take a moment to reflect on the changes you want to make and the new opportunities that await you.

The Apophis Club Draconian Magic Series

APOPHIS
Ægishjálmur: The Book of Dragon Runes
Dragonscales
Draconian Consciousness
Words of Power
The Grimoire of the Sevenfold Serpent
Gods and Monsters
Runes of Mann
The Sevenfold Mystery
Everything and Nothing
Runes of the Valiant
The Satanic Dragon
The Serpent's Promise
Rune-Shifting and Tarot Transformations
The Magical Vision of Anton LaVey

The Draconian Quadrilogy (the first four books above in a single, large format volume)
The Apophis Lectures: Lectures 1-25

Become a Patron

To become a patron of Michael Kelly and The Apophis Club, facilitating the production of more books and booklets such as this one, sign up and make your pledge at this website:

https://www.patreon.com/user?u=3389166

Not only will you help to fund the Draconian Great Work, you will also gain access to all manner of magical tuition available only to patrons. Depending upon your subscription level (as little as $5 for the podcast lectures), you can gain access to some or all of the following:

- A series of half hour lectures on magical topics. At the time of publication of this book, there have been 126 such lectures, with new ones added every month.
- A series of tutorial videos, covering magical subjects, with demonstrations. A new video is added every week.
- Skype discussions and tuition.
- Your name acknowledged as a patron in future publications.
- Participation in carefully crafted occult courses.
- Receive all future Apophis Club publications upon release as part of your subscription at higher tiers, with the option of signed copies.

The Patreon system provides the opportunity for these more direct and personal methods of tuition in a manner suited to the Twenty-First Century.

Printed in Great Britain
by Amazon

27806150R00106